Dec. [illegible]
Ray-I hop[illegible]
To do this together.
Thanks for your Friendship,
Mike G.

John Day River

Drift and Historical Guide

By Arthur Campbell

for
Raft
Drift Boat
Canoe
Kayak

Frank Amato Publications
P.O. Box 02112, Portland, Oregon 97202

ISBN 0-936608-11-0

Printed in the United States of America.

*To those settlers whose spirit and
determination contributed to the settling
of our western lands.*

TABLE OF CONTENTS

Introduction

As you drift the John Day and learn its recent history, you will see why this guide was written. There is much misinformation about this river, and perhaps the information between these two covers will help the reader to respect this river as the author has. The John Day River is as exciting and charming as any northwest river and probably ranks first in scenery and unspoiled beauty. Although the river is over 200 miles long, including its tributaries, this guide will deal specifically with the most commonly drifted section—Service Creek Bridge to Cottonwood Bridge—116 miles.

The John Day was named for a fur trapper and hunter who came to Oregon in 1812 with the Astor-Hunt overland party. The party had to split up in what we now know as Wyoming, due to a shortage of food and game. Each party was to seek its own way through to the Columbia River. Day and another man named Ramsey Crooks were separated from their party and wintered with some friendly Indians. They left for the Columbia River early that spring.

A few days later, one of the other parties came through the area and forced the Indians to give up horses and provisions. Enraged, the Indians caught up with John Day and Crooks, stripped them of everything including their clothing, and left them to the elements. Day and Crooks were found in near starving condition by others in the Astor party near where the river enters the Columbia. The river had been named by Lewis and Clark in 1805 The Le Pages after one of their French boatmen. The Indians knew it as the Mah-Hah. The John Day name has been in common use for about the last 175 years.

The author is indebted to many for their contributions to this guide. Contributors include Giles French, Annie McDonald Cloer, Francis Clarno, May McRae, Katherine Maurer, Van and Tom Rietmann, Ernie Fatland, Jack Steiwer, Lester Reinhart, Alex Hardie, Zack Keys, Vance Shearer, Al Starns, Shirley McIntosh, Dorothy and Martin Zimmerman, E. R. Jackman, Ione and Wayne Furniss, Ladd Zastoupil, Howard Walp, Gary Hendrix, Roger Leatherman and Val Darby. A special thanks goes to Sid, Doris and Sam Seal for lots of help and information; and to Kim Campbell for photographic lay-out assistance.

The material for this guide took nearly six years to compile and organize. Information was gleaned from recollections of old-timers who lived on the river, newspaper stories from the *Fossil Journal*, the *Condon Globe-Times*, and the *Antelope Herald*. Even a 1928 silent film made on the river helped some pieces fall in place.

Assistance is acknowledged from the following publications and materials: "Glimpses of Wheeler County's Past," F. Smith Fussner, editor; "Oregon River Tours," John Garren; "U.S. Army Map Reading Field Manual"; "Under the Shadow of Black Rock," by Anna May Bills Wright; "Topographic Maps, U.S. Geological Survey"; John Day maps—Bureau of Land Management, Prineville, Oregon; and "Over My Shoulder," by W. W. Weatherford.

The validity of some of the river yarns and stories may cause some concern for the readers, but if any fabrications or embellishments were added, it was long before the author heard the story. Stories were written as they were told and researched. You and history may be the judges.

Planning Your Trip

Planning doesn't make a trip, but lack of planning can cause a potentially good trip to be less enjoyable. If you are drifting the John Day for the first time, getting to the water and putting in can be considerably more difficult than you can imagine. If there is more than one vehicle going, plan to leave together and arrive together. A "We'll meet you there" approach can lead to problems for drivers who have not driven the roads and who do not know the area. If you are planning a car shuttle and want to estimate your time, a good rule of thumb for the distance shown on the area map on page 11 would be about a 20-minute drive for every inch of road on the map. In eastern Oregon when roads are straight, they are really straight, and when the map shows wiggly lines, the road is really crooked.

If you are coming from the Portland area, the quickest way to Service Creek and Twickenham would be through Wasco, Condon and Fossil (see an Oregon highway map). If you are coming to Clarno for a lower river drift, you will probably want to leave a shuttle vehicle at J. S. Burres State Park where Highway 206 crosses the John Day. It is still shorter to continue on to Clarno rather than trying to go back to Highway 97 through Moro, Grass Valley and Shaniko to Antelope. If you are coming from the Willamette Valley or the south and heading for Service Creek or Twickenham, Highway 26 out of Prineville would be best. If you are going to Clarno from the Willamette Valley or south, Highway 97 through Redmond and Madras would be best. There is a cut-off going to the right towards Antelope about 7/10ths of a mile or so above the Willowdale store, which is paved and shorter than going through Shaniko.

You may wish to do a car camp (or RV) the night before you start to insure getting on the water early the next morning. Self-contained RV's are more versatile, and there are hook-ups available in Condon and Fossil. J. S. Burres State Park on Highway 206 is little more than a gravel parking lot with privy, located in the middle of nowhere. Shelton Wayside Park between Fossil and Service Creek is the best camping park. It is green, sylvan, and in the pine trees. Dyer Park below Condon and The John Day Fossil Beds National Monument park near Clarno have no overnight facilities.

The River

The river flow is probably the most important consideration in floating the John Day. It can be negotiated by boats from 1500 c.f.s. (cubic feet per second) to about 4,000 c.f.s. All landmarks, island checkpoints and drift times in this guide were compiled when the river c.f.s. was between 2100 and 2400. Water above 2400 c.f.s. will cover the bars and some beaches making some checkpoints impossible to see. Drift times will also be altered. The river c.f.s. is measured daily at the Service Creek gauging station which is operated by the Northwest Water Resources Data Center in Portland, Oregon (telephone 503-249-0666). Call this number a week or so before you leave on your trip, and a day before you leave. This will give you the rate of change and help you know what you will face when you get there.

Extreme caution should be used when boating this river. The boater needs experience, and the best drifting time is usually late spring when the c.f.s. is between 2100 and 2500.

The river in most years is too low to drift after the 25th of June. The water is high in March and April, but the weather can be cold and windy. The lower John Day is usually not recommended for canoes. The author knows of two experts who turned over, and several canoes that were lost in the Clarno Rapids and the Great Basalt Canyon area (see page 49).

The main factor on the John Day, in addition to the water depth and flow, is the wind. If there is going to be a wind (it will nearly always blow upstream) it will come up in the afternoon, usually after 1:30 or 2:00 p.m. It is advisable to get in the water early and make your decision to camp, depending upon the weather, later that day. Rain squalls are frequent enough to warrant having rain gear handy. Sometimes wind and rain dictate a change of plans.

Below, a cut-away drawing will explain how the John Day can appear so treacherous at one time and so calm several months later. No dams control it, as does the Pelton on the Deschutes, and the river is subject to rise and fall with the snow melt, flash floods, etc. We know a party that drifted the lower river early one summer at 2100 c.f.s. and returned a year later to face an 8100 c.f.s. torrent. Needless to say, again several boats overturned in the Clarno Rapids (RM 105 to 104) and in the Great Basalt Canyon area (RM 94 to RM 90.5). Large boulders make the water very picturesque when the river is low, but extremely treacherous when water is high.

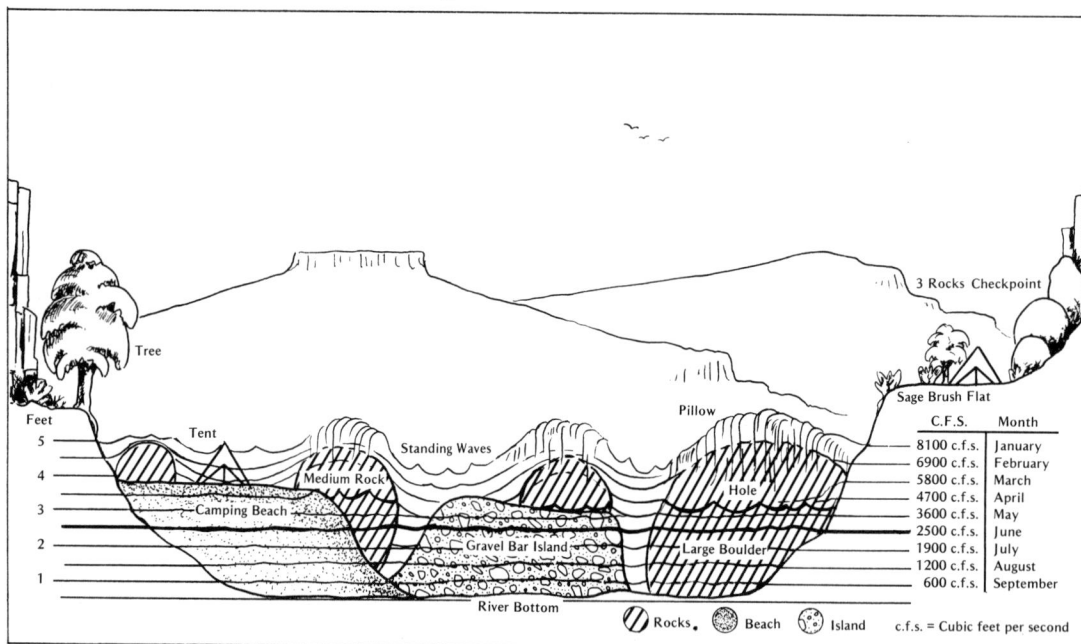

The above sketch shows the water level and corresponding c.f.s. flows in a hypothetical 9 month period. It is important to know the c.f.s. before you drift. Each of the above parallel lines equals 6 inches in river depth. See below.

Picture, if you will, a section of river about RM 92, which you visit in January, then each month until September. Note the c.f.s. readings next to each month on the right. Now look on the left side and see the difference in feet between the September level and the January level. You will note a five-foot difference. For every foot of depth, the river c.f.s. increases dramatically. Note the river bottom features. In June, the large boulder is half out of the water, the top of the island is a gravel bar with a large rock showing, and you could tie your boat behind the medium-size rock and find a great camping beach just above. If you came back a year later and the c.f.s. was 8100, the only campsite would be the sagebrush flat on the right. All the rocks and the island would cause much surface turbulence and possibly a Class IV rapid would result. The large boulder now has two feet of water running over it, creating a "pillow" on top falling into a hole or reversal four feet below. This could be extremely treacherous to the boater who can't see it from upstream. The water level on the left extends to the base of the tree over the previous year's camping beach. The only visible checkpoint might be the three rocks landmark (upper right), and you might be so busy with the rapids, you could miss it. The average drop in river flow in the spring is one to two inches per day. The river seldom rises again once it starts to drop. Don't make your trip so inflexible that you can't change it if the water and c.f.s. are too high for safety.

The John Day is protected as a wild and scenic river under the Oregon Scenic Waterways Act. Most of the land in the more remote sections of the river is controlled by the Bureau of Land Management. Almost all of the land under cultivation is in private hands. There is some concern by ranchers, especially in the Clarno area, about drifters. They realize that they cannot control who is on the river, but cars parked on private property, blocking gates, fires and constant streams of requests for use of the phone, etc. get very tiring from the rancher's point of view. When contacted, they are usually friendly, but reserved, due to the inconsideration of some of those who preceded you.

One Memorial Day Weekend, there were estimated to be nearly 1,000 people on the river between Service Creek and Cottonwood. This was established by the huge number of cars at the put-in and take-out points. If you leave your car at any of these points, be sure it is not on private property, not blocking gates and not obstructing traffic. The most convenient places to put your boat in or take it out are at the Twickenham Bridge, Burnt Ranch Rapids, Clarno Bridge and the Cottonwood Bridge (State Park there); or 1/8 of a mile up river from the Service Creek Bridge, your car should be safe, but do not leave valuables in it. The Service Creek Trading Post or Jim's Chevron in Wasco can arrange, for a price, to transport your shuttle car to any of the take out points. (See back cover for details.) Two adult wages must be paid and costs for an additional car to bring the driver back will be included. Call first and get a quote. It is your privilege to put in and take out at other than recommended sites, but you should clear this in advance with private land owners along the river.

Your Personal Gear

If you have been drifting for a while, this may seem redundant, but there are some items needed by all drifters on the river. A brimmed hat (with tie-down) is a good thing to wear. The sun is merciless to those that are not protected. Sun glasses, sunburn cream and lip balm are often used. Experienced boaters know that feet often get wet. We suggest tennis shoes or old jogging shoes, fishing boots (short) and something comfortable and dry for the camp. Unless you use hip boots, you can't keep your feet dry in a raft. Hard-bottomed boats are easier to keep dry in. The light shoes are recommended for the little white water there is, (in case you go into the river) but several different types of footgear are advisable. The author now carries hiking boots (after a truck broke down and the party was forced to walk 7 miles uphill on a rocky road). A kerchief or bandana around the neck will help keep the sun off.

Camping Sites

There are two general types of camping areas on the John Day: beach camps and what are known as sagebrush flats. The beach camps are far better, especially for the boats. There are more beach camps in the Clarno to Cottonwood section than in the Service Creek to Clarno drift. The main advantages of a beach camp are (1) usually driftwood nearby, (2) boats can be beached, unloaded and loaded easily, (3) fires can be controlled better and (4) camp is generally cleaner. The disadvantages of a beach camp are lack of shelter in bad weather, unavailability when you are ready to camp and dampness on the low beaches.

The sagebrush flat offers (1) some shelter (cattle shelter there too), (2) some privacy (between tents and bed rolls) and (3) more frequency along the John Day. The danger of fire is greater on the flats, and the cheet grass puts little sharp dart-like affairs in your socks. Beach camps are cleaned each year at high water, but you do see more signs of other campers on the sagebrush flats. Nearly every flat has been camped upon and you will see fire rings of previous campers. There are less beaches exposed earlier in the drifting season than later as the water lowers. The guide points out mostly beach campsites on the Clarno to Cottonwood drift as they are more numerous. The Service Creek to Clarno drift points out both. Most of the land (except under cultivation) is government land and you may usually camp where you wish, but knowing where good campsites are helps you set some tentative goals while you are drifting.

Camping Gear

One must for each party is a shovel. This is especially handy for those who tramp off into the brush for a latrine stop. When you get there, cover up your sign, including toilet paper with dirt or sand. Someone from another party may camp near there. Please follow the rule of the wilderness—leave as little trace as possible.

Cooking is an individual matter. Some use fires and some use portable stoves, depending upon the space in your boat and number in your party. Everyone usually wants a campfire, so you may wish to do both. If you use a stove, there is hardly any cleaning outside of pots to do. If you do have a campfire, whether you cook on it or not, pack out your garbage; don't leave it burned or unburned for the next camper to deal with. The best rule of thumb at a campsite—leave it better than you found it. This way all can enjoy it. Put out your fire with water and cover it with sand or dirt. Turn over smoldering pieces of wood and douse them again.

Some sleep in the open; some like tents (mosquitos are seldom any problem on the John Day). If you are an experienced camper, you have a preference. Remember, setting up camp requires the time to take it down. Whatever you use, make it easy to pack and unpack so you can get an early start on the river. The sun usually shines on the river canyons by 7:30 or 8:00 a.m. You should be on your way by then.

Simple meals that do not require much clean-up are best; one-dish meals are good and filling. Keep lunch materials handy so you can get at them easily for a lunch stop. Take a grill and broil your meat; cook other things previously frozen in pre-wrapped foil. The author often has cantaloupe and uses the shell for a cereal bowl to save time in the morning.

If you take an ice chest, you may have ice for 36 to 72 hours. Solid ice lasts longer than cubes or chips. One good way to keep things cold is to freeze square gallon or larger containers of ice water or your favorite water base drink. Place these in the bottom of your ice chest; place perishable items around or on top. Cover this with ice cubes and close the ice box. The cube ice will melt in 24 or 36 hours, but you will still have your partially frozen jugs to keep chilling your perishables up to 72 hours or more. As your liquid melts, you will also have clean cooking water and cold drinks. If you do not take an ice chest, you may cool canned soft drinks in the river by placing them in an onion or gunny sack and hanging them over the side. Cut a slit below where you tie the top off so you can reach in easily. You will need approximately one gallon of liquid per person every 24 hours. This includes soft drinks, cooking water, drinking water, etc. Most drifters boil coffee and dish water from the river. One tip—when taking any kind of liquid, always use a screw topped container and use as little glass as possible. Backpacking and outdoor stores carry many very satisfactory plastic products for these needs and uses.

Packing your gear is important. We see and hear a great deal about how strong this or that plastic bag is on TV. *Don't believe it!* On a river trip, bags are sat on, thrown on sharp rocks, snagged on trees, etc. Use these plastic bags to line other more durable bags, such as the ones you find at outdoor or surplus stores. A so-called water-repellent bag sitting in the bottom of a boat can soak up water like a sponge. Keep bags that are not totally watertight off the bottom of the boat. Get bags with handles and rings that can be tied down. A good way to check to see how waterproof a bag is, is to hold it up to the light and look inside. If you see light through the seams, it is not water tight. Special river bags sold at boat shops are excellent. Some canoeists use the 5-gallon plastic cans obtainable from most bakeries. These cans also have handles and tight-fitting tops. They also make good camp stools around the fire.

When loading your boat, it is important to keep the center of gravity low. Most gear in a raft should not be closer to the bottom than 4 or 5 inches. Be sure there is an air mattress or some kind of floatation device between the bottom of your boat and any hard items, such as an ice box or wood platform. When your boat goes over rocks this cushion is necessary to protect the bottom of the craft and keep your gear dry.

The hard, open boats, such as canoes and driftboats, may take in some water during your drift. Thin strips of wood spaced an inch or so apart and placed on the bottom of your boat act as a secondary deck and keep all gear low and dry. The John Day is not the Colorado and 95% of all wet gear was either stowed too close to the bottom of the boat in a non-water-tight container or fell overboard because it wasn't tied down. Keep all gear in some kind of container with a handle; tie all gear in containers securely through the handles. When you get to your camp, you may have to carry it up a steep, rocky bank and you will be glad the handles are there. There is nothing more pathetic when making camp than to see boaters struggling up a steep bank with plastic bags (all the same size and color) preparing to make camp. Once they get the bags ashore, they can't find anything because all the bags look alike.

You will encounter some spray in the few rapids the John Day has, but never enough to get any high baggage so wet that it won't dry out in a few minutes. The water repellent nylon bags are ideal for the top of your load. Keep one bag handy but well secured for a jacket, rain gear and other personal items you may wish to use from time to time. A good rule of thumb about baggage and gear—*if you value it, tie it down.* More gear is lost in shallow water by being knocked off of, or out of a boat than is ever lost in turbulent water.

All gear of any kind that is used should have a snap so that it can be hooked back in its proper place after use; this would include your bailing bucket, seat cushions and *anything* loose. 100 feet of good rope should also be included with your equipment.

Rain gear is a must. It should be packed in a bag easily accessible. The best outfit for boaters is a two-piece pants and top with a hood. Stay away from the cheap plastic suits and ponchos. The plastic suits have several disadvantages; (1) they tend to tear easily at stress points, (2) they act as a portable sauna and produce more water on the inside than they repel on the outside, (3) they stiffen when they get cold. The best gear is the northwest steelheader's outfit or the nylon backpacker's top and bottom. The heavier gear is warmer though, and rain on the John Day is sometimes accompanied by wind and cold. Ponchos with hoods are satisfactory for passengers (the Army surplus poncho is a very good buy), if used with some kind of waterproof pants. Don't skimp here; rain gear is not needed often, but when you need it, you need it bad. The comfort of your trip depends upon staying dry, so come prepared.

Safety on the River

Much of the safety in any drift lies with the knowledge and skill of a boatman. If the boatman is able to do the right thing at the right time, you will have a relatively safe trip. There are, however, precautions that you can take to minimize dangers if emergencies do occur. There are basically two types of accidents that can happen on the water: a boater may be knocked overboard or fall from the boat, or the boat may turn over and everyone goes in the water, including gear. If you boat long enough, either may happen to you or someone in your party. What can you do ahead of time? (1) Always wear your life jacket in turbulent water; (2) keep hard objects like metal boxes (some use these for camera storage) away from the right or left side of the boat, where people may go overboard (especially on rafts). When you go in the water, you want as little between you and the water as possible, so there will be no injury before you enter the water; (3) keep all bow, stern lines and painters in small coils or balls tied off so there is no loose rope longer than a foot in your boat—innertube rubbers are good for this. You may keep or attach one near the front and rear in your boat. Coil up the rope in a small package and tie it off. You will find that your lines will always be handy and not in the bottom of your boat getting tangled in gear, feet, etc. Use floating line or rope for your craft. When a boat turns over, cotton and nylon tends to sink and float around where your feet dangle. If you do fall overboard or the boat turns over, stay with it unless the boat goes into turbulent rapids or rocks where you may be injured. If all members of your party are O.K., stay with the boat until you can get it ashore. Look around for gear, hats, paddles, oars, etc.—all gear will float near the boat and at approximately the same speed as you or anything else in the water. Be sure, if you are in a raft, that a safety rope goes completely around your boat. This is advice that you will appreciate if one or more of your party goes into the water or if your boat overturns. If this happens, there is no place to hang on. You have a far better chance to stay with your boat if it has safety lines.

Rafts are a very forgiving craft. They can bounce off rocks, bluffs, and even other boats. They can and sometimes do go through rapids backwards or sideways. A raft, 95% of the time, will make it through turbulent water regardless of what the oarsmen do. When we say stay with the boat, this is excellent advice for rafters. As a matter of fact, staying in a raft can keep it from turning over. If your raft goes up on a rock or some obstacle at a severe angle, just lean or stand uphill and your weight will usually cause the raft to slide down from whatever it was hung up on, with only some water in the boat to worry about. Many inexperienced boatmen or passengers panic and go into the water as they fear being trapped under the boat. If you lean or stand uphill when the boat takes on any disturbing angle, it will help the oarsman or paddlers recover quickly.

Life vests for each person in your boat are required by law. The John Day is for the most part a very quiet river, but there are some rapids where life vests are a must. Keep them handy and wear them in all turbulent water. Only a rank novice who thinks nothing can happen to him disregards their importance. The waist belt type is fine for water skiers waiting for a motor boat to pick them up, but are inadequate for fully clothed drifters in the water. The standard horseshoe collar type will float an unconscious wearer head up, but they are uncomfortable especially in hot weather, and the plastic lining encasing the kapok inside tends to break if these vests are sat upon in the boat or around camp. A medium-priced preserver and one most commonly used on the river is the complete vest type which has a closed-cell foam (PVC or polyvinyl chloride) encased in a nylon shell. They offer more protection because they have a full back, especially in turbulent water and rocks. If you buy this type, be sure and get one with adequate outside pockets for miscellaneous small gear you will need on the river. Another type, usually expensive, is the vest made of segmented plastic air tubes covered by rip-stop nylon. Whatever type you use, adjust it snugly on your body so that it doesn't move up once you go in the water.

Don't let your aquatic skills lull you into complacency concerning safety. Going in the water is a shock, even to the most experienced boatman, and before you go into the water something has usually happened—you hit something, your boat overturned, an oar or paddle was lost or broken, etc. This panic, combined with cold water and concern for the safety of others and gear, can cause you to go into varying degrees of shock. The more precautions you take for this event, the less likely it will happen, but when it does you will be as ready as you can, if you take the above precautions and use common sense.

Below you will find four of the standard rapids classifications used to rate the John Day water. There are four basic things to watch for (1) velocity and depth of water, (2) height of standing waves, (3) obstacles and (4) turns in the channel. Often it is easy to cope with one or two of these conditions; but when they occur three or four at a time with high velocity water, difficulty may be encountered. Rapids are rated by a combination of difficulties and many of the serious problems are caused by rocks, boulders and cliffs at water's edge. At Russo, Homestead and Burnt Ranch Rapids there is high velocity water running into or near cliffs. Homestead and Burnt Ranch Rapids also have turns to negotiate, in addition to boulders above and just below the water line. The conditions at all rapids vary with the time of year and scouting is advisable for the novice in these waters.

Let's discuss briefly the terms novice and expert. Many people confuse the word expert, with a natural skill such as can be found on athletic fields and courts. Skill in your craft may be connected with natural ability, but all beginners are novices until they have experience. Only those with experience can pass through the intermediate stage to expert. Experts are those who have read the water correctly, carefully considered and recognized the dangers and have done the same thing many times. Conquering danger may give one an exhilarating feeling and some valuable experience, but the expert has had enough training to recognize and minimize danger. That's why he is successful.

Class I   Easy

Sandbanks, bends without difficulty, occasional riffles with waves regular and low. Boater should use care to avoid obstacles such as gravel bars, sandbanks, etc. River speed less than hard back paddling or rowing. Velocity 0-6 miles per hour.

Class II   Medium

Fairly frequent but unobstructed rapids, usually with regular waves, easy eddies and easy bends. Course generally easy to recognize. River speed occasionally exceeding hard back paddling. Speed velocity 2-6 miles per hour.

Class III   Difficult

Manuevering in rapids necessary. Small falls, large regular waves covering boat. Numerous rapids. Main current sometimes sweeps over or near obstacles. Course not always easy to recognize. Current speed usually less than fast forward paddling speed. Velocity 4-8 miles per hour.

Class IV   Very Difficult

Broken water, long extended rapids. High standing waves, eddies and abrupt bends. Course often difficult to recognize. Scouting usually necessary. Swift current and rough water experience indispensable. Velocity 10 miles per hour or more.

The John Day seldom reaches a Class IV except during flood stage. Spray covers for hard boats, especially canoes, advisable in Class II, III, and IV water. Most John Day rapids are in the II to III category.

How to Use the Map and River Guide

The maps usually appear on the left-hand side of the guide. The scale is approximately 1:24,000 for all maps except the area highway map on page 11. In simple terms the 1: means one unit or 1 square on the map. The 24,000 indicates that the square on the map equals 24,000 times that unit on the actual ground.

Some symbols will be used on a number of pages. See below:

(RM 158)	△ 26m	(48.3)	[Hartman Drowning 1899]
River Mile	**Minutes from last checkpoint**	**Point of interest between river miles (in tenths)**	**Special Landmark**

The river in the upper section (Service Creek to Burnt Ranch) generally runs from east to west, and it is more difficult to place maps so they can be read when they go across the map pages. After the Burnt Ranch rapids, the river generally runs south to north and you can point the guide downstream and also see the dialogue and drift times easily. Always read the east to west maps from right to left. Occasionally, more than one will cross the map page; read the top one first and then go to the bottom section. If you watch the river miles closely, you shouldn't have any difficulty. Each map section will always have a start and end printed at each end to help you. All map information is printed so it can be read if you point the guide downstream with north facing the top of the page.

The actual river scale and canyons entering the John Day are reasonable facsimiles of the 7.5 minute and enlargements of 15 minute Department of the Interior topographic maps.

Note: As the John Day flows towards the Columbia River, miles are counted in reverse, but the tenths are easier to count forward.

Example: Between river mile 110 and 109 you will find:

110.1   110.2   110.3   110.4   110.5   110.6   110.7   110.8   110.9

The river meanders through the one mile grids on the map pages and the symbols used for each drift can be found on the first map page of that section.

On the dialogue and river time pages, you will find 4 columns for raft, driftboat, canoe and kayak. Each has a different drift time. If a raft and kayak leave from the same point, the kayak will get there much faster over a given stretch of water. Use the column for your boat each time you calculate where you are and the time it takes to get there. The small m stands for approximate minutes, so 16m on the chart equals 16 minutes. These times were calibrated on average days, medium water and no wind. Many variables can change the time it takes to drift from one checkpoint to the next, and these times are very general and can vary 10 minutes in every 30 minutes, depending upon water and wind conditions.

To the right of the drift columns is the historical narration, with checkpoints. There are two types of checkpoints you will be concerned with: *island and landmark* checkpoints. Islands do change somewhat, but landmarks along the shore are usually permanent.

There will be timed checkpoints if you care to estimate where you are. When the words *island checkpoint* or *landmark checkpoint* appear, the dialogue will tell you what to look for. The river mile in an oval or circle will tell you where to look on your map, and the numbers inside the triangle will tell you the raft drift times from the last timed checkpoint. More rafts drift the John Day than any other type of boat, so in the triangles are raft times. You may choose to jot down your times near the triangles, or read your times from the chart on the right-hand page. Circles (river miles) and triangles (drift time) will usually be across the river from each other, space permitting. The rectangles will appear from time to time and are points of interest; some may be checkpoints, many will not. All island checkpoints are timed from the center of the island. We have tried to keep the river mile checkpoints and points of interest opposite each other so that you could always see the appropriate map section to the left of the printed dialogue, river mile and drift time page. This was not always possible. Mountains are merely general location indicators and are sketches; they are not to scale, but elevation will be printed for those mentioned in the dialogue.

The islands are the most unreliable of the checkpoints. Some appear and disappear depending upon the height of the water. Some may have flowing water on both sides. Some may have had flowing water on the backside (the side away from you) but the river has gone down and now there is mud or gravel where the water once ran. A dry island that no longer has water around it will look like a bar extending out from shore. Several things give away a dry island: (1) dried algae and dead moss on rocks where water covered them earlier in the year, (2) a bank above the island and towards the land side indicates water passed through there, (3) damp moist ground with fresh green vegetation, and (4) driftwood and fine sticks, lodged in any growth or trees that may be on the island or bar.

At high water, the island may disappear entirely or become a shoal that you may drift over. If there is any vegetation or rocks, this may be visible above the waterline. Small willow trees and branches protruding from the river are a certain indication that an island of some sort has been covered by high water.

If you miss an island checkpoint, there are enough landmark checkpoints downstream for you to get your bearings together. The guide and maps may seem a little confusing to use at first. All printed information on each map page is best read as you point map downstream. As you drift, you will see the guide become more valuable and informative with each mile.

You may wonder about the names of places and landmarks along the river. The author asked this of the government people responsible for making the official topographic maps. Their answer was that field men talking to locals will usually name landmarks what two or more property owners on both sides call it. All canyons, high ground and some rapids were named this way. The author has taken the liberty to name some river landmarks for drifters' reference points. Such names as Hungry Rock, Cathedral Rock, Arch Rocks and Cave Bluff, to mention a few, are not official names, but if they stick perhaps some day they will be.

FISHING

The historical reports on fishing in the John Day are a conservationists nightmare. About 1889 a dam was placed across the river at Early to supply power for a grist mill. Before that time, salmon came up the Columbia and spawned in the John Day River and its tributaries.

Some oldtimers recall stories of "harvesting salmon with pitchforks in Butte Creek" and making fish traps of willow sticks and chicken wire. The dam is gone now and until 1971 the river was populated with what the locals call trash fish—suckers, squawfish, some carp and small bullheads. Sporatic runs of steelhead in the fall and early winter months was about the extent of fishing on the river.

About 65 to 75 smallmouth bass were placed in the river in 1971. These fish thrived and multiplied throughout the 116 mile drifting section in this guide. They can also be found above Service Creek and below the Cottonwood Bridge. Fishing for these bass is an art and requires some experience and skill. Fishing gets better as the water clears in early June. Six to eight-pound test line is recommended and some successful bass lures have been rapala lures, rooster tails and other small spinners. Small diving plugs will reach the deeper holes. Jigs and weighted worms are often successful if worked along the bottom. One fisherman in the late seventies caught a daily limit on a 1/16 ounce Mr. Twister jig. Small minnow and safety pin lures may also be used.

The most productive locations for bass have been the deep holes in April and May. As the water warms up and clears, good fishing can be found below riffles, along rocky shores and sand bars with weeds and rushes. The average size bass caught is from 1 to 1½ pounds. Larger fish can go up to 3½ to 4½ pounds. If you are not an experienced bass fisherman, talk to someone who can give you good advice. These fish are not easy to catch but are there for the taking for those who know what they are doing.

AREA MAP OF JOHN DAY AND NEARBY TOWNS

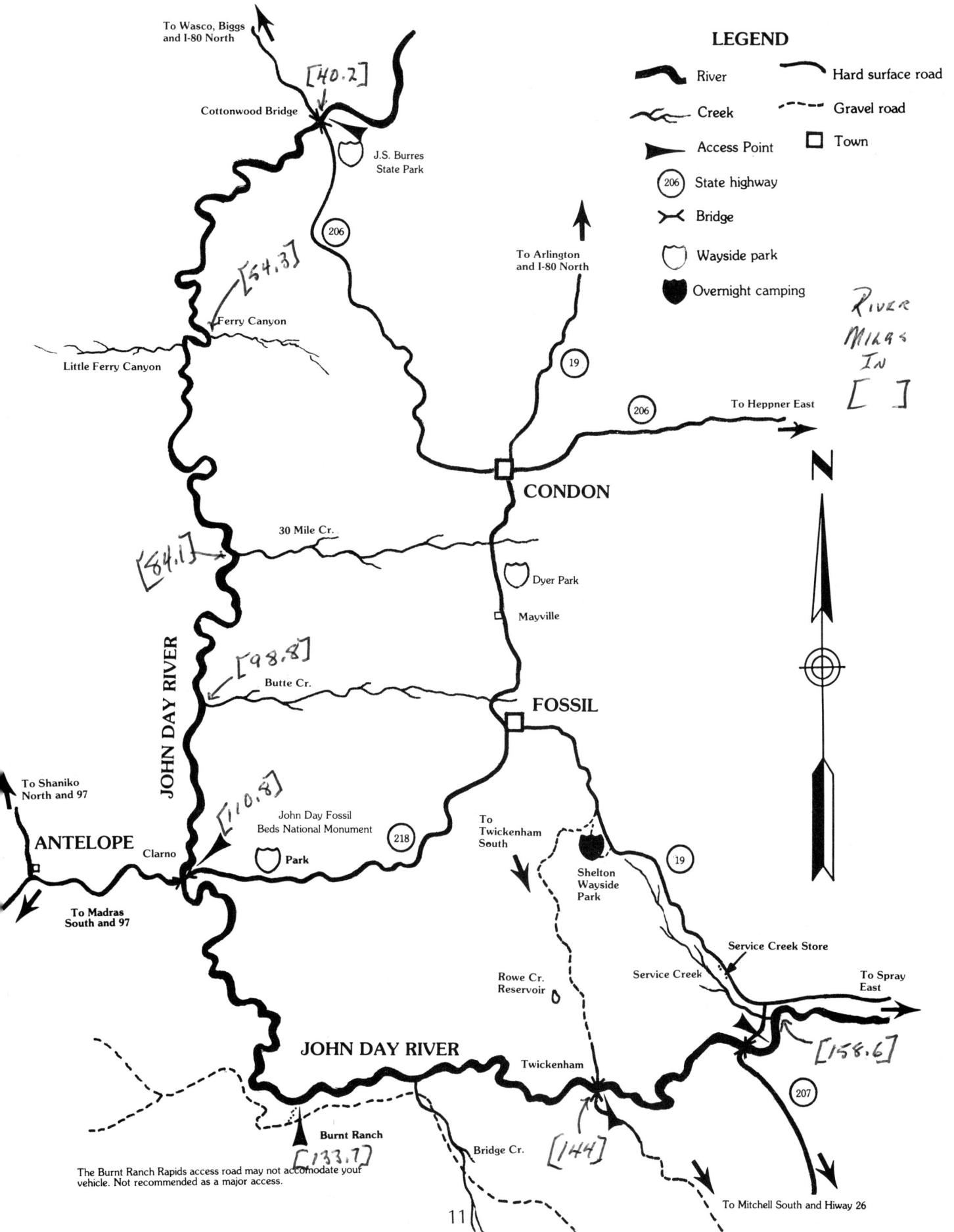

LEGEND

River		Hard surface road	
Creek		Gravel road	
Access Point		Town	
206 State highway			
Bridge			
Wayside park			
Overnight camping			

To Wasco, Biggs and I-80 North

[40.2]

Cottonwood Bridge

J.S. Burres State Park

206

[54.3]

Ferry Canyon

Little Ferry Canyon

RIVER MILES IN [ ]

To Arlington and I-80 North

19

206 To Heppner East

CONDON

30 Mile Cr.

[84.1]

Dyer Park

Mayville

[98.8]

Butte Cr.

FOSSIL

JOHN DAY RIVER

To Shaniko North and 97

[110.8]

John Day Fossil Beds National Monument

218

To Twickenham South

Shelton Wayside Park

19

ANTELOPE

Clarno

Park

To Madras South and 97

Service Creek Store

Service Creek

To Spray East

Rowe Cr. Reservoir

JOHN DAY RIVER

Twickenham

[158.6]

207

Burnt Ranch

[133.7]

Bridge Cr.

[144]

The Burnt Ranch Rapids access road may not accommodate your vehicle. Not recommended as a major access.

To Mitchell South and Hiway 26

11

Note: Overnight accommodations can be found in Condon and Fossil. Biggs Junction has restaurant, gas and motel accommodations. You may find restaurants and gas at Service Creek and Antelope. These places usually close by 7:30 p.m. Restaurants and gas stations in Condon and Fossil may not be open after 8 or 9 p.m.

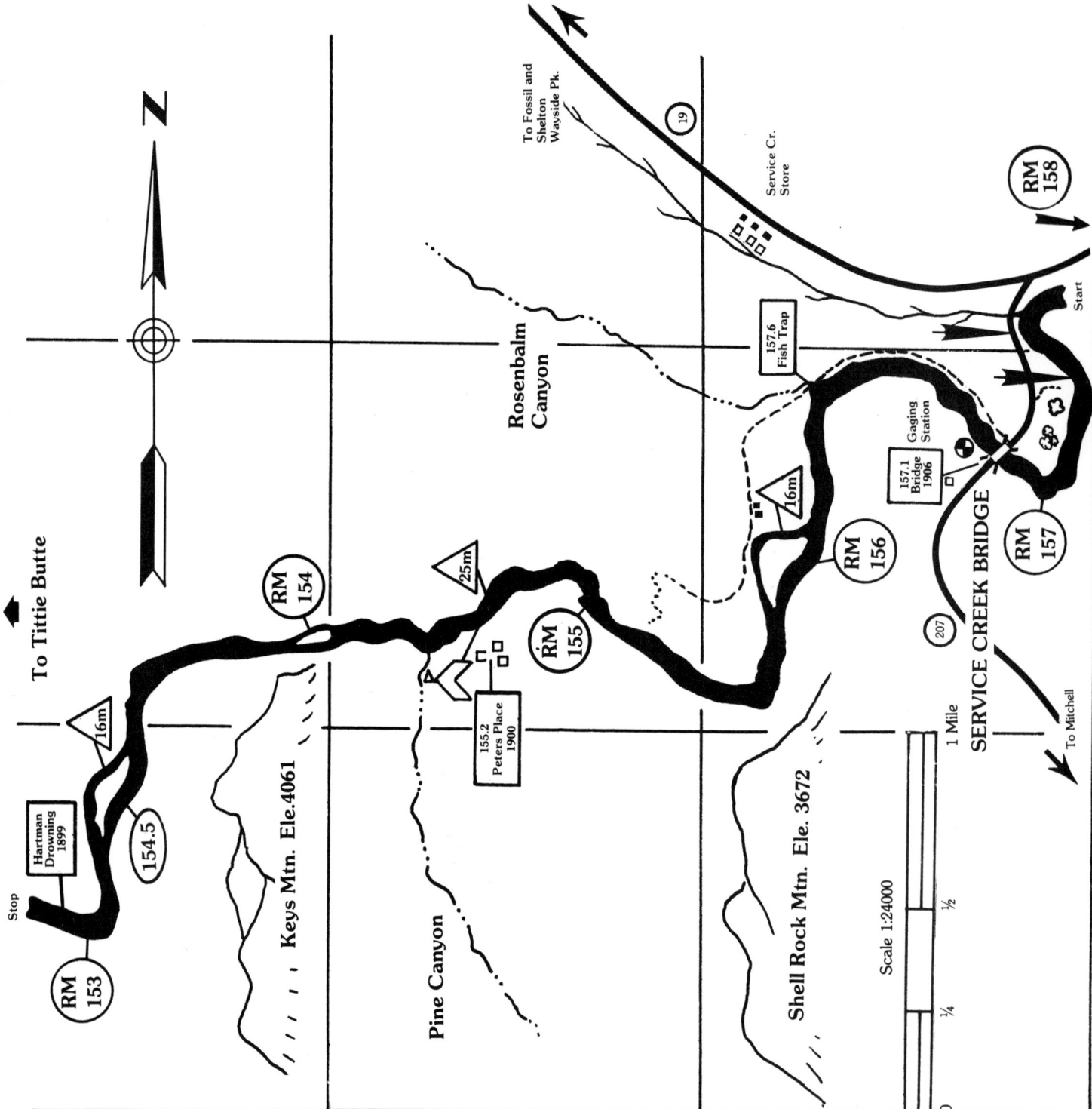

N

To Tittle Butte

Stop

RM 153

16m

154.5

Hartman Drowning 1899

RM 154

25m

155.2 Peters Place 1900

RM 155

Keys Mtn. Ele. 4061

Pine Canyon

Rosenbalm Canyon

16m

157.6 Fish Trap

To Fossil and Shelton Wayside Pk.

19

Service Cr. Store

RM 158

Start

Gaging Station

157.1 Bridge 1906

RM 156

RM 157

207

To Mitchell

Shell Rock Mtn. Ele. 3672

SERVICE CREEK BRIDGE

Scale 1:24000

0   ¼   ½   1 Mile

LEGEND

Hartman Drowning	Special landmark
19m	Minutes from last checkpoint
RM 158	River miles
60.3	Point of interest between river miles (in tenths)
	River and islands
	Creek (usually wet)
	Canyon (usually dry)
	Rapids or rough water
	Riffle
	Pond or lake
	Hard surface roads
	Gravel roads
	Jeep trails or pack roads
	Bridge
218	State road designation
	River access
	Unoccupied structure or barn
	Occupied structure
	Partial structure
	School
	Campsite near
	Trees
	Gaging Station

SERVICE CREEK TO TWICKENHAM

DRIFT TIME

KAYAK	CANOE	DRIFT BOAT	RAFT	RIVER MILE
10m	11m	13m	16m	

River Mile: 158.6 to 144 (14.6 Miles)

Estimated Drift Time	Recommended c.f.s.* 1400 to 4000
Raft . . . . 3.5 to 5.5 hrs. Drift Boat . . . 2.5 to 4.5 hrs. Canoe . . . . . . 2 to 4 hrs. Kayak . . . . . 2 to 3.5 hrs.	Times to the left are estimates and reflect **time on water only.** More accurate times this drift can be found on page 20.

158.6 **Putting in at Service Creek.** There are two possible options—from the junction of Highway 19 and Highway 207 (¼ mile below Service Creek Store) turn onto 207. Immediately on left just a few yards beyond where Service Creek enters the John Day is a turnout. Another possibly better option is about ¼ mile towards the Service Creek Bridge. Here there is a large open area on the left with a sandy but rocky beach.

157.1 As you leave from either area the first prominent landmark is the *Service Creek Bridge.* Swing wide above bridge to select best path around the two supports, both of which are in midstream.

This bridge was once called Sarvice Creek (origin of name unknown). Ferry crossed near present bridge site, placed in service about 1889. Replaced about 1904. Water so high here in 1906 mail had to be sent across ferry cable in a coffee can. An Indian was hired to swim across to get rig working.

157.3 .1 of a mile below bridge on the left is the Service Creek Gaging Station operated by Geological Survey Northwest Water Resources Data Center.

157.6 As you start to sweep left at the head of some fast water, it was here that man named George Williams had a fish trap made of willow sticks and chicken wire about 1890. The trap was left unattended for several days so that many fish got trapped and destroyed the trap. Such traps were made illegal in 1905.

157.9 Ranch on right, low flat island ahead, is first checkpoint. Take left channel when water is high. High ground ahead is called Shell Rock Mountain. Believed to have been named for ancient shell fossils found there in early days. Elevation 3,672.

156 **Island Checkpoint.** (Check your time here against time at left to see if river is faster or slower.) Difference between your time and time on left should be constant for remainder of trip.

---

*c.f.s.=cubic feet per second. See page 1 for more details.

DRIFT TIME

KAYAK	CANOE	DRIFT BOAT	RAFT	RIVER MILE	
15m	17m	20m	25m	155.2	**Landmark Checkpoint.** Buildings on left are the old Peters place, built about the turn of the century. Peters sold property to Malcolm Keys in the late twenties. Hay and alfalfa were raised in what is now a sagebrush flat. To the left of the house, sheep and cattle were also raised. Good camping on left. Both Malcomb and his wife could tell funny stories about their life on the property.

The Mrs. claimed that any baking products during the depression years, that didn't turn out right, could be dumped in the river and only the fish would know. It seems that a batch of bread didn't rise to expectations; she baked it anyway, then decided to dump it in the river. It promptly sank!

Malcolm had an embarrassing and painful experience while irrigating about 1932. Some wild bees got inside his pant leg. As he was about to remove his pants, a car load of women happened along the road on their way to a meeting his wife was holding at their home. He said the stings were too painful for him to leave his pants on, but it was too embarrassing to take them off!

Keys was elected Wheeler Co. sheriff in 1941, and remained in office until 1972. After the 1941 election, Keys and his family moved to Fossil. The house was inhabited by successive sheep herders who used house and grounds for a sheep camp until about 1950. If you stop there—wear boots—there are some rattlesnakes in the area.

As you look downstream, the prominent high ground to the southwest is Tittie Butte, El. 2800 ft. The butte becomes invisible behind some bluffs and then reappears beyond some short minor rapids about ¼ mile downstream.

The hunting was good here and there were lots of deer killed here in the early days. A story about the name of this butte has an interesting twist. It seems that a government man years ago sent in to Washington the recommended name of Squaw Butte (locals knew it as Squaw Tit Butte). A typing error in the report made the name read Squaw Butt. The supervisor in Washington wrote back to his field man that he would accept the Squaw Butt name, but he didn't think it was appropriate for a map. The error was corrected and the name Tittie Butte remains. There is also a Squaw Butte several miles down stream.

14

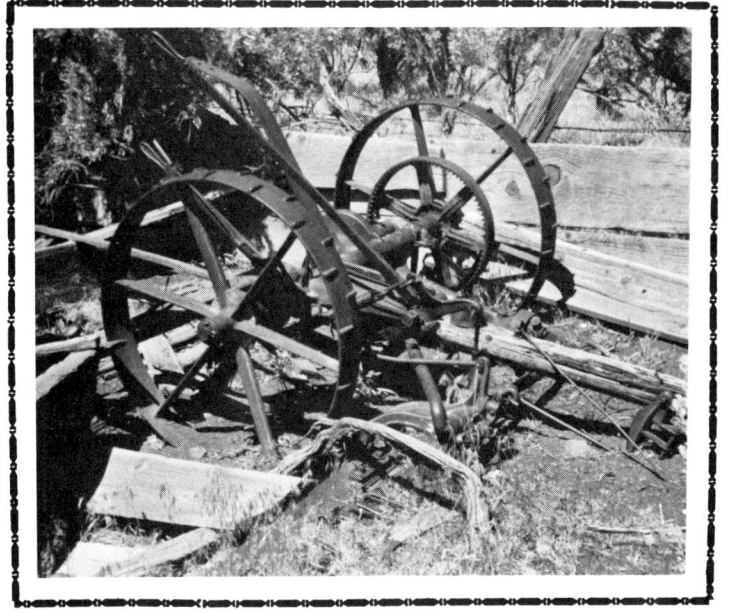

Old Peters Place: Built about 1900, this house and adjoining land was home and farm for two families in the early days. A man named Peters raised a family here and then sold it to Malcomb Keys in the late 20's. Keys later became Wheeler County Sheriff. There are several out-buildings standing and fallen in, rusting pieces of machinery and farm equipment on the grounds. In its later years until about 1952, it was used as a sheep camp. Apparatus at the upper right is the remains of an old hay mower.

Big Juniper Flat Ele. 3969

N

Deer Canyon

Russo Rapids

151.9

151.4

RM 150

RM 151

152.9
Dugout
1896

RM 152

Rowe Williams Canyon

Start

Tittie Butte

60m

Shoofly Canyon

Keys Mountain ele. 4061

Camel Hump Ele. 3590

150.9

Tap Horn Canyon

RM 149

25m

Clark Canyon

RM 148

Stop

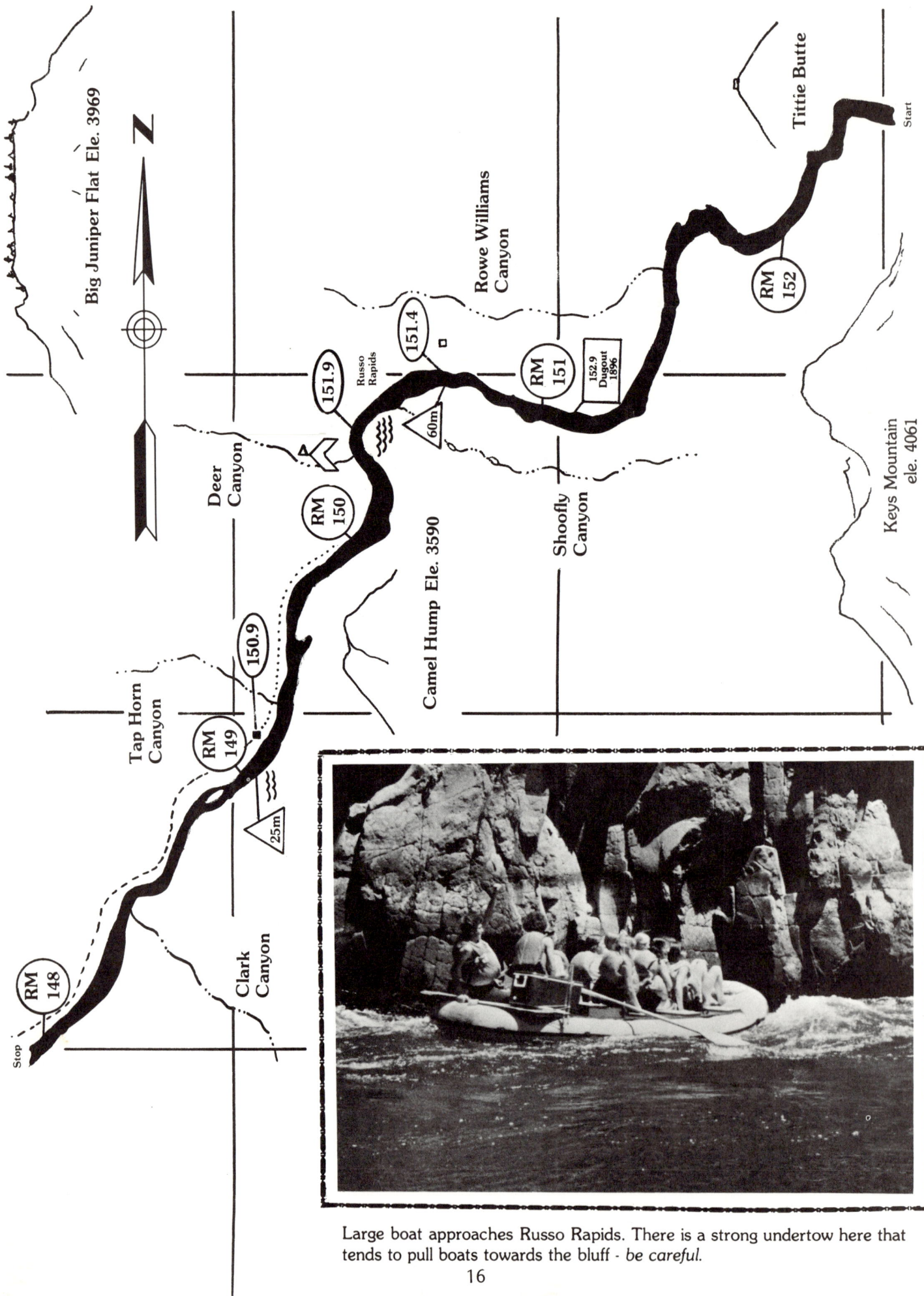

Large boat approaches Russo Rapids. There is a strong undertow here that tends to pull boats towards the bluff - *be careful.*

16

DRIFT TIME

KAYAK	CANOE	DRIFT BOAT	RAFT	RIVER MILE	
10m	11m	13m	16m	154.5	As you leave the Keys building the river jogs slightly and runs straight for about ¼ mile. Then the river turns due south with another island checkpoint ahead. The high ground around the bend ahead is Keys Mountain, elevation 3,504. Take left channel; this is an **Island Checkpoint.**
				154.9	As the river makes a sharp turn south approximately ¼ mile below last checkpoint, this is where a man named Hartman drowned about 1896 on the north side of the river.
				154.4	Coming in from right is Rowe Williams Canyon, named for an early settler.
					High ground in the distance is Big Juniper Flat, elevation 3,969. As river makes a sweeping left turn south again at the next bend is where a man lived in a dugout from about 1896 to 1917.
				152.9	A dugout was a house partially dug into the hillside, usually very crude with dirt floor. This structure was on the right side of the river but is no longer visible. The old Butler homestead was about ¼ mile to the north, also.
					End of Keys Mountain dead ahead.
37m	41m	48m	60m	151.4	Here can be seen an old cabin on right bank. As you drift in front of cabin this is an **Island Checkpoint.** This checkpoint is 2 to 4 minutes away from the head of Russo Rapids.
				151.5	Shoofly Canyon on left. In the winter of 1875 Indians were camped up Shoofly Canyon. They had little food and were starving. Mr. R. R. Russell and Zack Taylor Keys loaded up some pack horses with food and took them to the Indian camp. Russell and Keys were running sheep just across from the canyon on the south side of the river.
				151.9	Russo Rapids comes directly at an oblique angle into a short bluff. There are two main hazards. Boats too far left can go against bluff and when river is low, large boulders just under surface can hang up some craft. Enter rapids from right center if water is high enough, avoid bluff; there is a strong undertow here. If you can "cheat," try to cut inside of main current. Russo would be classed as an intermediate rapid—class II or III depending on water flow and level. Line right if so inclined. Good beach and backwater below and to right of rapids. Also good camping and lots of firewood.

17

To Shelton
Wayside Pk.
Highway 19
and Fossil,
North

Stop

Kentucky Ridge

James Canyon

Squaw Butte Ele. 3819

RM 144

RM 145

146.9

RM 148

Start

55m

RM 147

15m

TWICKENHAM BRIDGE

45m

RM 146

Dead Dog Canyon

N

Girds Creek

To Highway 207
and south to
Mitchell

Horse Mtn. Ele. 4266

Scale 1:24000

0   ¼   ½   1 Mile

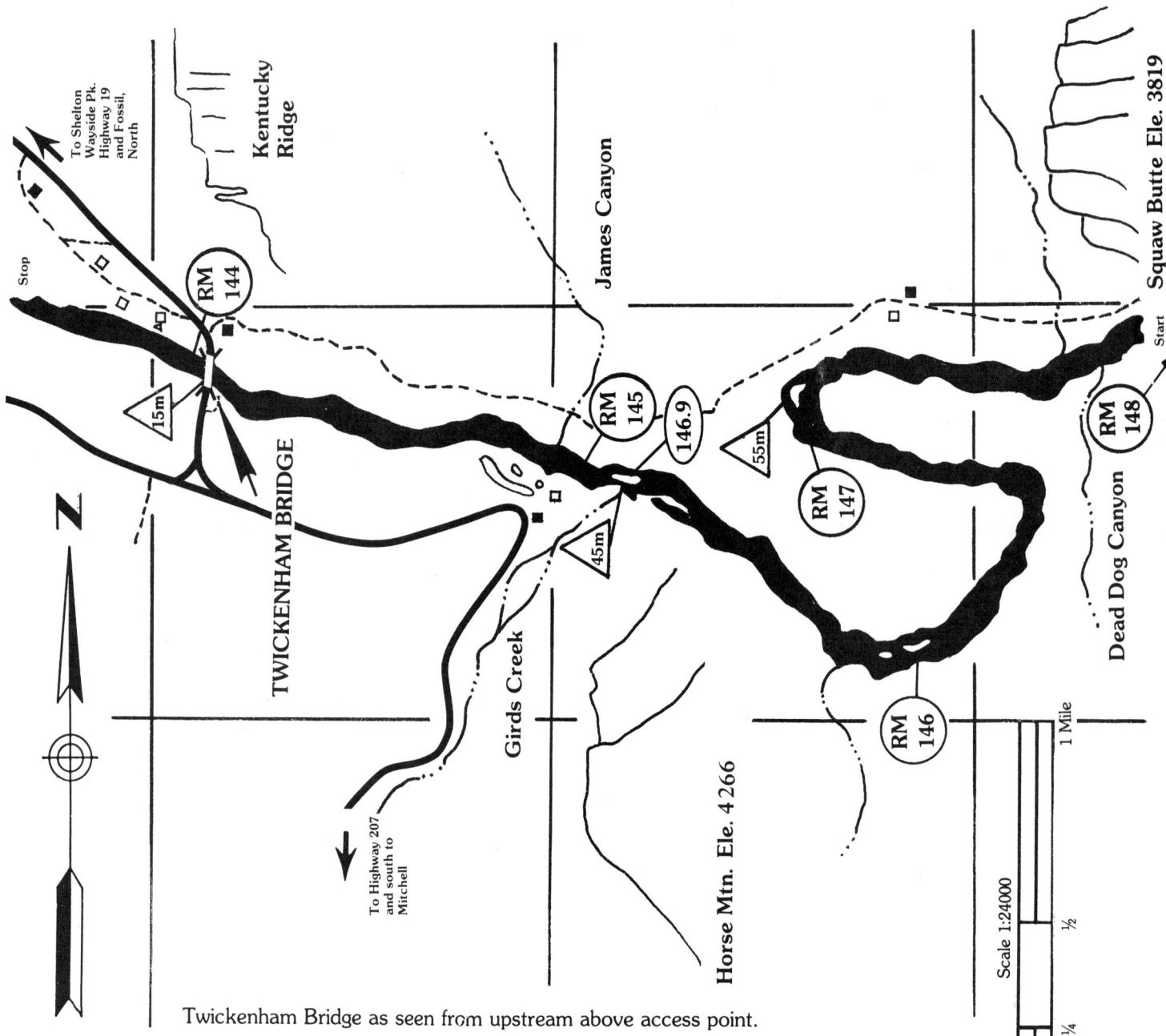

Twickenham Bridge as seen from upstream above access point.

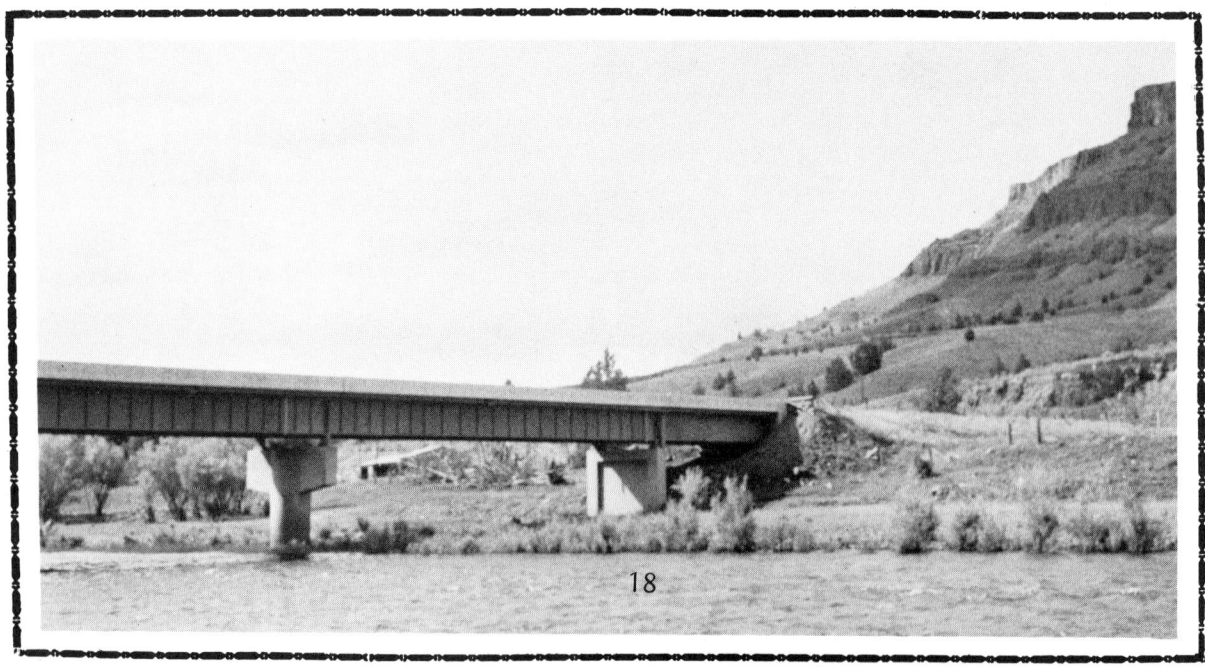

18

DRIFT TIME

KAYAK	CANOE	DRIFT BOAT	RAFT	RIVER MILE
15m	17m	20m	25m	150.9
				147
				149.1
34m	37m	44m	55m	147
28m	30m	36m	45m	146.9

About ¼ mile downstream below Russo Rapids to the left is a domed mountain with a slight ridge down the middle called the Camel Hump, elevation 3,590. In the far distance down river is Horse Mountain. The highest point on this mountain is 4,266 feet.

Tap Horn Canyon on right is named for early settler of that name. Nearly one mile from Russo are some minor rapids with a ranch on right. This is **Landmark Checkpoint**. An island is about ¼ mile below the rapids.

Ahead on right is the south end of Squaw Butte. These flat-topped rocks eventually lead up to a 3,819 foot butte 1¾ miles to northwest (butte out of sight now). The name origin is as follows:

The story goes that an Indian had 5 squaws and he was collecting and tanning deer hides in the area around 1875. The hunting was good and the squaws did the tanning (a considerable chore). The squaws wanted to go to the Columbia River where other Indians were. The Indian turned out the horses near Jim Canyon so the squaws could not leave.

High ground ahead left is Horse Mountain, elevation 4,266. Coming down to the river between two peaks of the mountain is Dead Dog Canyon. On left Dead Dog runs into Trail Canyon about 1½ miles from the river. Trail Canyon is named for an old trail which ran to Richmond about 8 miles away. Old-timers in the area used it to get to the town and dances that were held there.

Beyond Horse Mountain can be seen another mountain with a rock spur jutting up. This is Pack Saddle Mountain, elevation, 3,508 feet. River makes gentle turn to right and then straightens out at the end of this ½ mile stretch. Ahead can be seen some corrals and an old house (new dwelling on hill). The island on the sharp bend is an **Island Checkpoint**.

After the checkpoint and you are into the center of the section of the S curve, look directly behind through a gap in the hills and you can see Kentucky Ridge. This landmark can be recognized from this angle by a sharp spur rising separately in front of the ridge, which runs north for about 3 miles. As you complete the S curve and the river straightens out, you are about 2 miles from Twickenham Bridge.

As you come to some welcome fast water there is an **Island Checkpoint** with the old Davis Ranch on the left. You should be able to see the bridge from just below river mile 145. The Twickenham Bridge is approximately 1 mile away.

19

DRIFT TIME

KAYAK	CANOE	DRIFT BOAT	RAFT	RIVER MILE
				145.1
				145.6
9m	10m	12m	15m	144

145.1 Coming down from Kentucky Ridge is James Canyon. Map makers got a little formal here, as the locals called it Jim Canyon. Upstream to the right is Horse Mountain; upstream to the left is a good view of Squaw Butte.

145.6 Old cabin on south side of river on road. Originally belonged to J. F. Asher who owned and ran the Twickenham Ferry in 1907, before the bridge was built. Cabin may not be visible from river. Harold Turner drowned near here in July of 1921. He was swimming with John Asher of Spray when he walked off into a deep hole and disappeared. He came up once but Asher was unable to help him.

144 The Twickenham Bridge, **Landmark Checkpoint**, was built in 1907 and replaced in 1917. Old concrete polings here and there were reinforced with old fence posts (posts still visible—see old pilings under and near bridge). Present bridge completed in 1972.

Twickenham was once named Contention because each neighbor "contended" for his own kind of public policy. Frankie Parsons suggested a name change after Twickenham, England. This area was also known as Big Bottom. A town was plotted here in 1896 and the first settler, Jerome Parsons, started ranching here by 1871. At one time, Twickenham had a post office, a ferry run by Parsons, a general store, hotel, and a blacksmith shop. The town once aspired to be the Wheeler Co. seat but lost out to Fossil 436 to 267 votes in a 1900 election.

Optimism seemed to be a way of life in the Twickenham area and great hopes were kindled when coal was discovered here about 1885. There was talk of a railroad and increased population. The coal was found to be of low grade and hardly worth mining. A dam was considered here below the bridge in 1909 for irrigation purposes. The Fossil newspaper's editorial advice that year was "Damit, Gentlemen, Damit." Nothing remains of the once thriving hamlet, but faded memories, great aspirations and the proud name of Twickenham.

SERVICE CREEK TO TWICKENHAM				TOTAL MILES
2:36	2:54	3:22	4:15	13

20

Twickenham — The Beautiful
By E. R. Jackman — 1957

The coyotes howl for Twickenham,
The bobcats prowl in Twickenham,
But do not go to Twickenham
If seeking dive or joint.
There is no jail in Twickenham,
There's little mail in Twickenham,
But I'd rather choose a Twickenhammer
For driving home a point.

Now no train runs to Twickenham
So to make a trip to Twickenham
You approach another city
You ask your way with prayer;
Some go by way of Antelope,
Or Waterman, or Shaniko,
But do not go to Lone Rock
You cannot leave from there.

I'd rather live in Twickenham
Than Amsterdam—or Rotterdam,
For they eschew profanity
From grandpa right on down
And if you'd stand right out in Twickenham
And boldly call out "Twickenham"
They'd cast you out of Twickenham,
They'd throw you out of town.

So it's "Oh to be in Twickenham,"
In Twickenham, in Twickenham,
It's Oh to be in Twickenham some frosty night in June.
For everything is spick 'n span
In Twickenham, in Twickenham
And I'd rather take a lickin' than
To miss a trip to Twickenham
Where the lambs and calves are singing and every one in tune.

Old house in Twickenham, built about 1898. Houses of this vintage that are still standing are used for grain storage or cattle shelters now. Buildings like this once sheltered families, through life's trials.

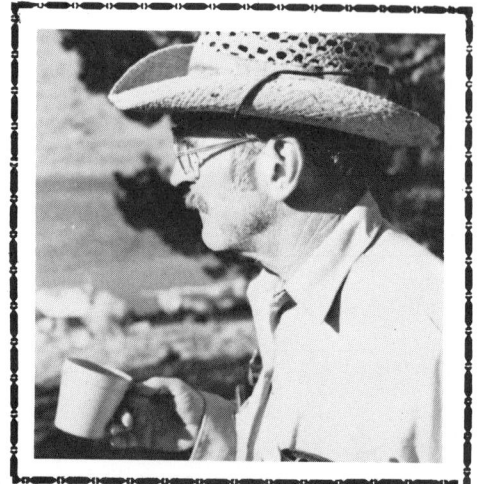

River Rat: Howard Walp of Portland State University with morning coffee, looking over the river. An early start is a good idea on the John Day.

Above left: Twickenham Bridge near access point. Note old fence post used as reinforcing in the 1906 concrete piling. Present bridge finished in 1972. Lower right: Old tree and wagon wheels silhouetted against the evening Twickenham sky. Below left: Canoeists putting in under the Twickenham Bridge.

22

Upper left: The remains of a range steer "that didn't winter too well." Right: One of several thousand tires illegally stored in a gully near Mitchell. Flash flood sent them all down the river about 1973. There were several law suits and counter suits over the affair. The property owner paid a fine and all was forgotten. Boy Scouts from Fossil drifted the river and took out what they could find. Below left: Boaters quietly drift while fisherman tries his luck. Below: Boaters in the Burnt Ranch Rapids skirt a danger spot.

23

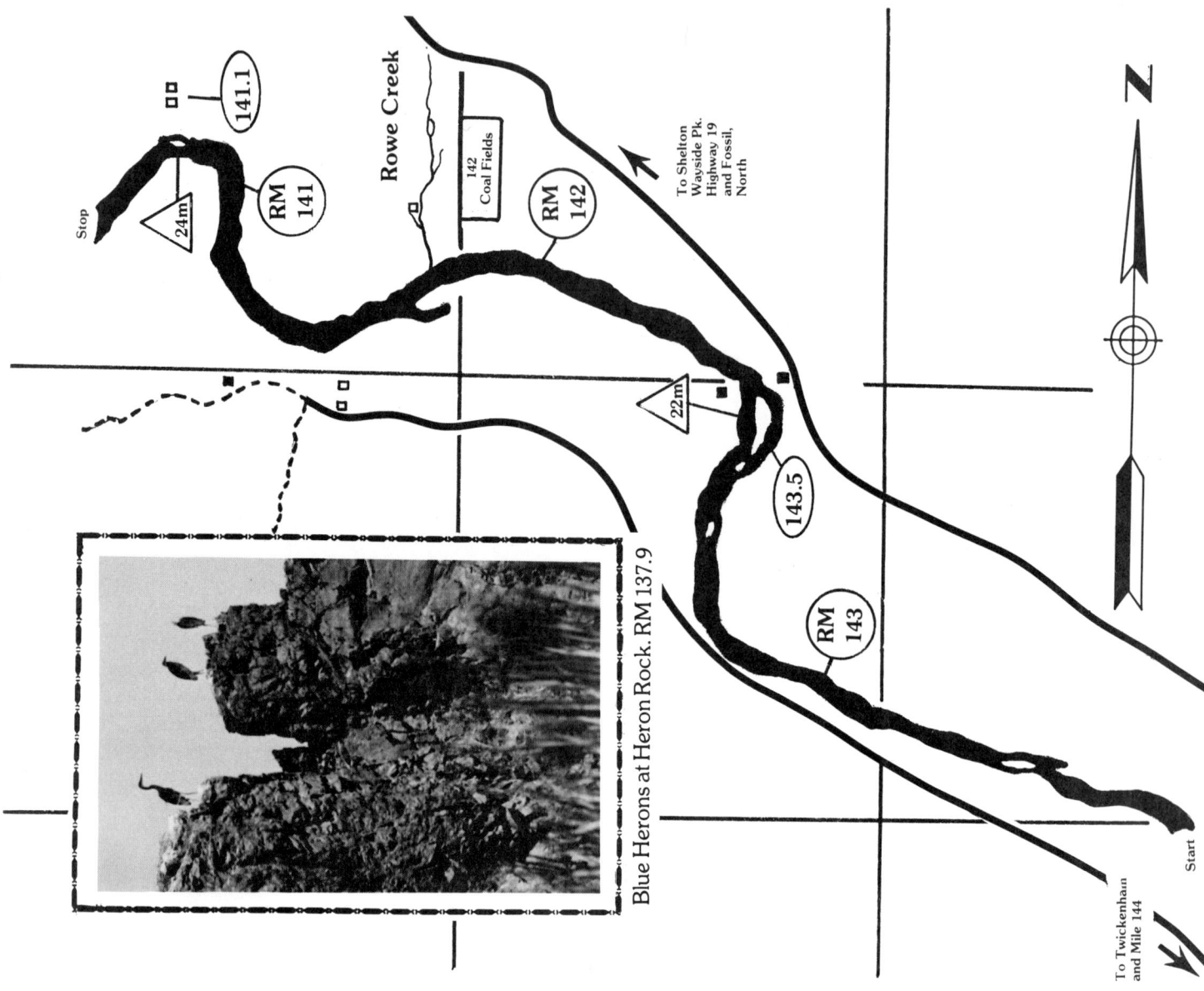

N

Stop

141.1

RM 141

24m

Rowe Creek

142 Coal Fields

RM 142

143.5

22m

RM 143

To Shelton Wayside Pk. Highway 19 and Fossil, North

Start

To Twickenham and Mile 144

Blue Herons at Heron Rock. RM 137.9

LEGEND

Liberty Bottom	Special landmark
26m	Minutes from last checkpoint
RM 158	River miles
90.5	Point of interest between river miles (in tenths)
	River and islands
	Creek (usually wet)
	Canyon (usually dry)
	Rapids or rough water
	Riffle
	Pond or lake
	Hard surface roads
	Gravel roads
	Jeep trails or pack roads
	Bridge
218	State road designation
	River access
□	Unoccupied structure or barn
■	Occupied structure
△	School
	Campsite near
	Windmill
	Trees
	Domestic powerlines

24

TWICKENHAM TO CLARNO

River Mile: 144 to 110.8 (33.2 Miles)

DRIFT TIME

KAYAK	CANOE	DRIFT BOAT	RAFT	RIVER MILE
				144
13m	15m	17m	22m	143.5
				142

Fut In 6/23/99 2300 cfs

Estimated Drift Time	Recommended c.f.s.* 1400 to 4000
Raft . . . . . 9.5 to 12 hrs. Drift Boat . . 7.5 to 10.5 hrs. Canoe . . . . . 6.5 to 8.5 hrs. Kayak . . . . 5.5 to 8 hrs.	Times to the left reflect **time on water only.** More accurate times for this drift can be found on pages 31 and 45.

144 As you leave the Twickenham Bridge you can see a high peak against the skyline to the northwest or the right. This is Jennie's Peak, named after the first young girl to move into the area. Andrew Clarno settled about 35 miles down river in 1867. Jennie, one of his children, was twelve years old at the time. As she matured into adulthood, she had her difficulties with men. Her first romance was with a riverboat captain whom she planned to marry about 1887. When his son showed up prior to the marriage, she discovered the good captain had not told her of the previous marriage. Jennie, heartbroken, called it off. A year or so later she married a contractor named Robb, but was only with him for a few months before they separated. She later moved to Portland and managed a hotel there and kept house for her brother, Charlie, who later committed suicide. She returned to Clarno about 1903 and built a 10-room hotel and rooming house. She left again about 1905 and the hotel was torn down in 1928, the same year Jennie died. It seems that fortune seldom smiled on Jennie, but the peak named in her honor remains a memorial to her pioneer spirit and pride.

Looking back up the river on the left is the entire Kentucky Ridge which is visible and is capped on the north end by a prominent landmark named Kentucky Butte, elevation 4,018 ft. Downstream on left the high ground is Sutton Mountain and the landmark for downstream with the knob is Byrds point. This is opposite Burnt Ranch.

143.5 **Island Checkpoint.** Ranch on right and ranch on left.

142 Twickenham Coal Fields—Early settlers discovered croppings of coal along the river bank and up Rowe Creek to north. It was tried out by blacksmiths and was found to be of poor quality. Mr. Jerome Parsons also discovered croppings up Dry Hollow. During the 1880's and 90's Charley Miller, a miner, came and tried to develop these mines. Parsons invested about $10,000 in the mines by 1905. The mines never panned out and Parsons died in 1906.

*
c.f.s.=cubic feet per second. See page 1 for more details.

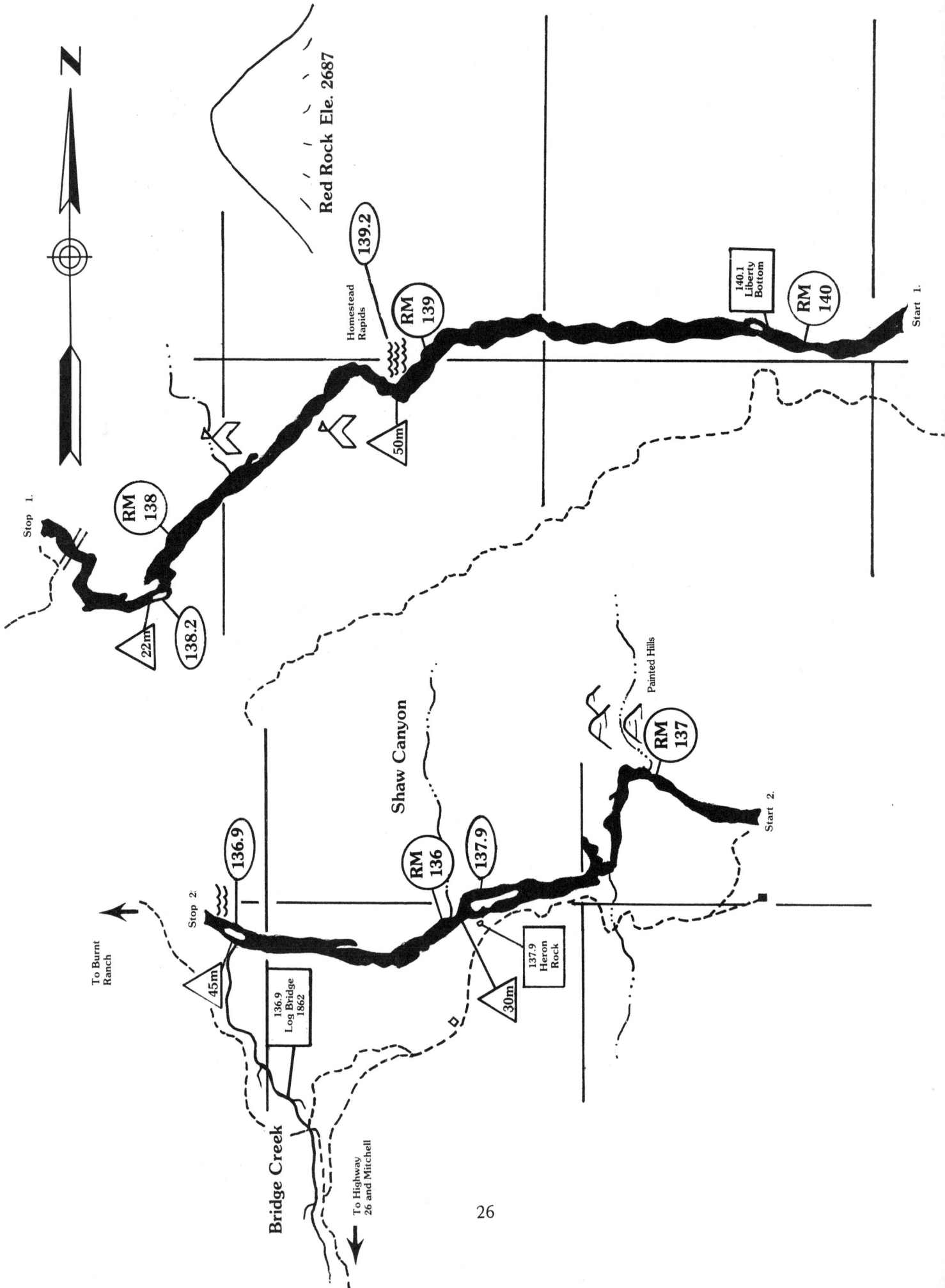

N

Red Rock Ele. 2687

139.2

Homestead Rapids

RM 139

50m

RM 138

22m 138.2

Stop 1.

Start 1.

140.1 Liberty Bottom

RM 140

Shaw Canyon

136.9

RM 136

137.9

Stop 2:

45m

136.9 Log Bridge 1862

137.9 Heron Rock

30m

RM 137

Painted Hills

Start 2.

Bridge Creek

To Burnt Ranch

To Highway 26 and Mitchell

DRIFT TIME

KAYAK	CANOE	DRIFT BOAT	RAFT	RIVER MILE
15m	16m	19m	24m	141.1
				140
31m	34m	40m	50m	139.1
13m	15m	17m	22m	138.2

6/23/99 Camped L Bank - Long way to Tree but good camp.

Ahead can be seen Red Rock, elevation 2,687 ft. and to the right along flat land near the river is a buff-colored strata of diagonal rock. This is a good fossil bed. Fossils in this bed date as far back as 66 million years. If you plan to stop, put in directly below old buildings on right which are the next checkpoint. There is good beach there, and the land is private.

A still was discovered under a bluff in August of 1922 on the left side of the river, 3 miles below Twickenham Bridge in thick brush. Sheriff Johnson and deputies found two drums, one 50 gallon gasoline barrel and one 5 gallon affair used as a finisher for the liquor. Two 50 gallon barrels of mash were destroyed also. One gallon of moonshine was also confiscated.

Old buildings at right are **Landmark Checkpoint** (also island at low water). As you leave the checkpoint you will have about a mile and a half of quiet water, and Red Rock is still the predominant feature on the right. Homestead or Fossil rapids are about 35 to 50 minutes away. Liberty Bottom on the right, thought to have been named during the Centennial Year of 1876, was settled by Zack Taylor Keys about then.

The approach to the rapids is signaled by the river turning slightly to the left around a bluff. As the river picks up speed in a fast riffle, stay left. Ahead is a sage and juniper flat in front of a pyramid-shaped rock. The river smashes into a small bluff from right channel. Keep left into quiet water. If you are a novice to these rapids, scout from bar on left. Entering rapids from left center when water is high is best route. Keep out of the right channel so your boat won't be swept into base of the bluff. Line left.

Homestead Rapids—Landmark Checkpoint. Many good camping areas for next mile, right and left bank. Rapids vary between class I, II and III, depending upon river. Below Homestead Rapids is a long quiet stretch of river which runs for one mile. As the river turns to the left there is an **Island Checkpoint.** As the river sweeps right there is a farm building ahead on left and some power-lines. To the left down river is Byrds Point. River makes a sharp right turn against small bluff. As you come from behind this rock into the main channel, you may experience some wind. Wind on the John Day frequently can be found just below such formations. Painted Hills are to the right. Red is caused by iron oxide in the soil, and the black is the result of volcanic ash settlement.

R ® Camp 6/25/98

27

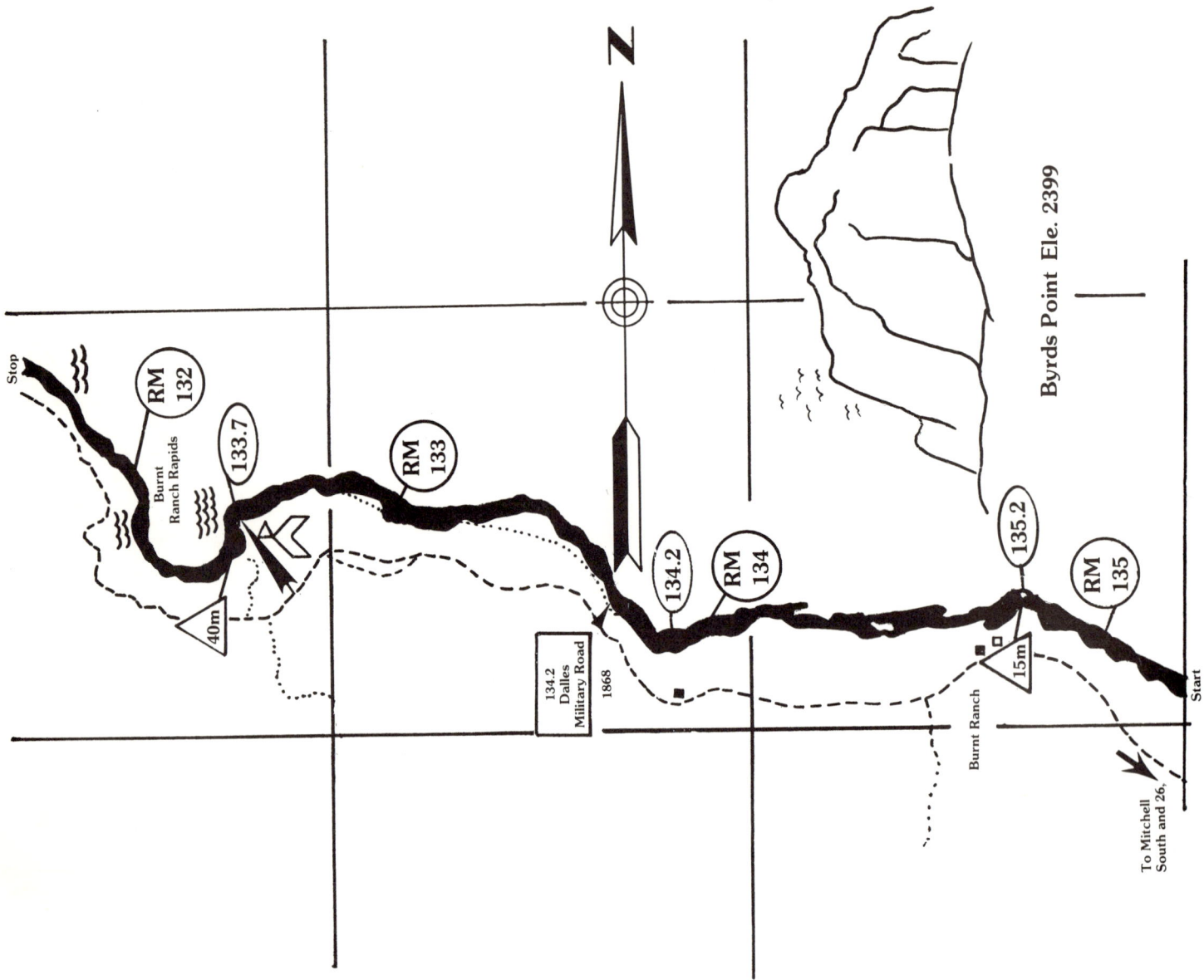

Byrds Point Ele. 2399

Stop

RM 132

Burnt Ranch Rapids

133.7

40m

RM 133

134.2

RM 134

134.2 Dalles Military Road

1868

135.2

15m

Burnt Ranch

RM 135

Start

To Mitchell South and 26.

Boater approaches Burnt Ranch. Rock on right is checkpoint 135.2. *(Story of Burnt Ranch on page 29-30)*

28

DRIFT TIME

KAYAK	CANOE	DRIFT BOAT	RAFT	RIVER MILE
18m	20m	24m	30m	137.9
28m	30m	36m	45m	136.9
9m	10m	12m	15m	135.2

Ahead is shallow water when river is high or several islands when river is low. Directly behind this point is a large flat-topped rock. As you near this area, keep looking to your left and you will see in a field a white-capped rock which has served as a nesting place for a number of generations for blue herons. Nest is white due to many years of bird droppings. Rock is on fenced private property. Flat rock ahead is a **Landmark Checkpoint**.

Back upstream Kentucky Butte can be seen on the left. River ahead for about ¾ mile is quiet and runs between two bluffs. Where bridge creek enters the John Day on the left is the beginning of some short minor rapids and on the left is an **Island Checkpoint**. Take right channel.

Bridge Creek got its name from a juniper log bridge constructed over it in 1862 by two California prospectors enroute to the gold mines at Canyon City. A post office was situated near here on the Al Sutton Ranch from 1868 to 1882.

Directly ahead is Byrds Point. This landmark, which has been visible since leaving Twickenham, is 2,399 feet in elevation. As you come directly opposite Byrds Point, there is a 15-foot high rock in mid-channel. This is a **Landmark Checkpoint**. The Burnt Ranch can be seen on the left.

This white house is not the original dwelling but was built about 1900 on the site of an older structure. Dwellings near this site served as a stage and way station for travelers in the early days (before 1910).

The story of Burnt Ranch is well-known in the annals of Central Oregon history. In September of 1865, James Clark and George Masterson forded the river near here to cut driftwood on the river bar opposite and upstream from the present house. They looked up to the south and saw a band of Indians coming down the hill at full gallop. The men were unarmed, having left their rifles at the cabin where the house now stands. Two work horses were unhitched from a wagon and the men made a dash for the cabin hoping to get there ahead of the Indians. They got across the river, but when they saw the Indians would get to the cabin first, they swerved back up river to Bridge Creek with the Indians in hot pursuit.

29

KAYAK	CANOE	DRIFT BOAT	RAFT	RIVER MILE

Masterson's work horse gave out as he headed up Bridge Creek. He jumped off the horse and told Clark to ride for help. Masterson jumped into the creek and swam downstream a short distance. He found a deep undercut beneath the bank hidden by brush and holed up there The Indians did not catch up with Clark or find Masterson. In the meantime, Clark had run on to a bunch of packers on the old military road and they returned in force to the area. On the way they found Masterson and proceeded to the ranch.

The Indians had ransacked the several buildings there, including the cabin. They took everything of value including the ticking material from the bed. What they could not carry off they burned, including the buildings. The place is called Burnt Ranch to this day, and is situated on the Old Dalles Military Road that passes along the river here. The Burnt Ranch checkpoint is 1¾ miles from the Burnt Ranch Rapids.

134.2 Below the white house at Burnt Ranch is another smaller dwelling on the left bank, opposite prominent outcropping of rock above the road on the same side of the river. The road comes down Bridge Creek from Highway 26 and goes to Ashwood and Antelope. Immediately below the present road is another old roadbed just a few yards from the river. This is believed to be part of the Old Dalles Military Road. Part of it is faintly visible along the river just above the water line to the left.

134.8 In the early 1860's, gold was discovered near Canyon City about 75 miles east of here. Many miners came to the "diggings"—some by riverboat to The Dalles where they were outfitted.

A pack trail from The Dalles to Canyon City came through this valley on the south side of the river. Later as Indian activity increased, military posts were established along the route. The nearest post was at Camp Watson about 40 miles southeast of here.

In 1868 the U.S. government granted to the Dalles Military Road Company every odd section of land within a six mile wide corridor for nearly 300 miles between The Dalles and Ft. Boise, Idaho. This land was to be sold at $1.25 per acre to settlers to finance the road construction. It was said that the final road consisted of 2 ruts 330 miles long which meandered around for no apparent reason except to acquire more land for the company. A scandal of major proportions was in the making. An inspection party headed by the then Governor of Oregon, George L. Woods, came to investigate the road in 1869. Road company officials apparently "wined and dined" the governor to the extent

30

DRIFT TIME

KAYAK	CANOE	DRIFT BOAT	RAFT	RIVER MILE
25m	27m	32m	40m	133.7

				TOTAL
TWICKENHAM TO BURNT RANCH RAPIDS				MILES
2:30	2:45	3:15	4:08	10.3
				TOTAL
SERVICE CREEK TO BURNT RANCH RAPIDS				MILES
5:06	5 hr.	6:37	8:23	23.3

that no changes or court actions resulted, and politics prevailed. Most of this land is now held by the Eastern Oregon Land Co. and little was ever sold to settlers. The old road comes into the valley between two high points of land due west of here. It turns up Bridge Creek towards Mitchell. Little of it is visible today and much of it is covered by present roads.

Warning for rapids will be a riffle near a little white rock and also a large rock below bluff at water's edge on right. Rapids are ¼ mile downstream. As you approach rapids, you will see a bluff downstream on the right. Just below this bluff, the rapids start, but there is quiet water above. Opposite bluff is a sandy beach, so stay left and aim for a rocky point with junipers above on left. Beach is just beyond if you plan to scout rapids. This is also a good camping beach, not much privacy though. Locals sometimes swim and picnic here.

Burnt Ranch Rapids Landmark Checkpoint. Rapids change with water level. At high water you can "cheat" the rapids by staying right and cutting inside the curve of white water. When river is lower right center is often used. Rapids drop some 10 feet in 100 yards. The main concern is submerged rocks which can only be seen from below and the bluff on left. Rapid class is II to III depending upon water level and flow.

There is little suitable camping ground for the next several miles. Most of the flat land is under cultivation. As you leave the Burnt Ranch Rapids, there will be about ¼ mile of riffles and minor rapids. Domed rock directly downstream is Wagner Mountain, named for an early settler. The high ground to the left is Domogalla Ridge and the cone–shaped peak on the right is Sand Springs Butte.

After several bends are turned at river mile 131 and 130, a large rock appears to be clasping a smaller one at river mile 130.5.

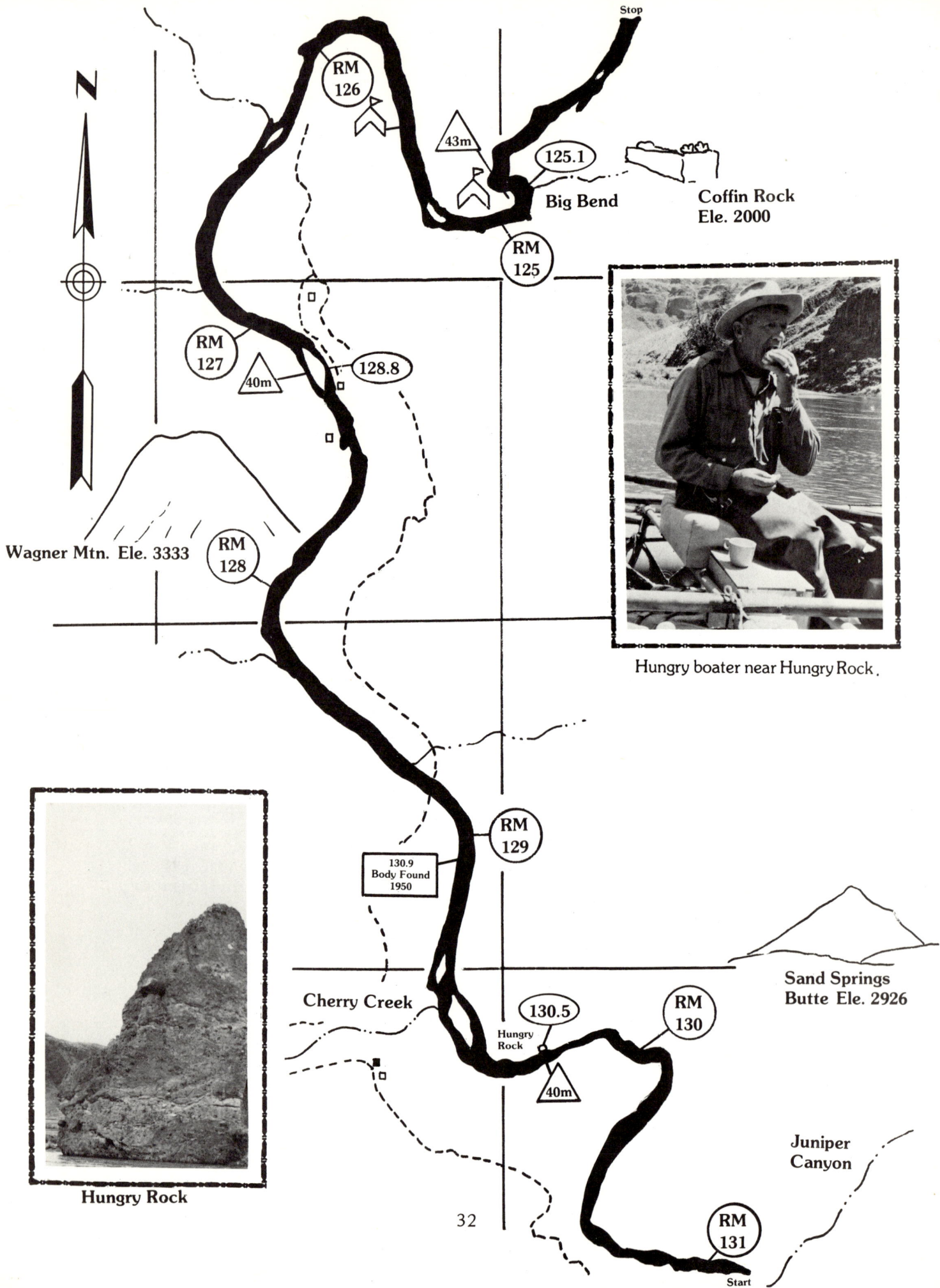

N

RM
126

43m

125.1

Big Bend

Coffin Rock
Ele. 2000

RM
125

RM
127

40m

128.8

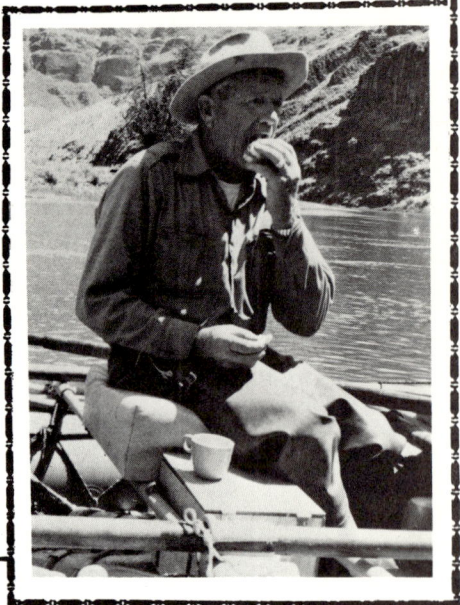

Hungry boater near Hungry Rock.

Wagner Mtn. Ele. 3333

RM
128

RM
129

130.9
Body Found
1950

Hungry Rock

Sand Springs
Butte Ele. 2926

Cherry Creek

130.5

Hungry
Rock

RM
130

40m

Juniper
Canyon

RM
131

Start

Stop

DRIFT TIME

KAYAK	CANOE	DRIFT BOAT	RAFT	RIVER MILE
25m	27m	32m	40m	130.3
				130.9
25m	27m	32m	40m	128.8
				127
				126.5
26m	29m	34m	43m	125.1

130.3 The author has named this landmark Hungry Rock. This is a **Landmark Checkpoint**, approximately 25 to 40 minutes from Burnt Ranch Rapids. In the distance can be seen Cherry Creek Ranch. As you turn north again there is a large long island. The island has two channels at high water. Coming in from left on the bank below is Cherry Creek.

130.9 A grisly find was made in 1950 by a man who came to cut firewood. He found the body of Kenneth Depu who had drowned some months before near Spray. The skeleton and parched skin, clad only in a belt, was found draped over some driftwood. The belt buckle aided in the identification.

About a mile downstream from Cherry Creek Ranch, the river will turn gently to the right. On the hill to the right is a road with powerlines. Directly ahead is a rock formation with a fan-shaped protrusion which is called Coffin Rock. (Some names may seem inappropriate as landmarks are viewed from different angles, but a mile or so ahead the rock does indeed resemble a coffin.) The mountain behind Coffin Rock is Coyote Mountain. Powerlines continue along the river. As you travel along parallel to the powerlines, a high peak on left reminds one of the statues and carvings found on Easter Island.

128.8 Below as two bluffs taper off is an **Island Checkpoint**. The north end of this island is opposite the Wagner Ranch. Buildings and corrals can be seen directly ahead as you round the bend.

127 The Wagner family settled here in the late 1880's. A private ferry was used across here for many years at high water. It is believed that at this point in December of 1897 the ferry overturned with the McWillis brothers and their father. The ferry was loaded with sheep. Men and sheep thrashed their way ashore with at least one McWillis boy hitching a ride on one of the sheep.

On the left side of the river are mountains belonging to the Melendy Ridge which connects with Wagner Mountain to the left which is 3,333 feet in elevation. (Mountain is not visible.) As you come around a sharp bend at mile 126.5, there is a long, quiet stretch of water with good camping on the right. After about ¾ mile of quiet water the river turns at a right angle to the left and runs below a high ridge on the right for ¼ mile. The river turns sharply left again in a "U"-shaped bend which is a **Landmark Checkpoint**. A good beach can be found at the bottom of the "U."

33

Spring Basin
Canyon

Hay Bottom
Canyon

119.9
Pictographs

119.8

Eagle
Canyon

Stop

35m

N

Sheep Mtn.
Ele. 3101

RM
119

Black Rock
Ele. 2115

120.1

Two boulders

RM
120

121.9
Jones Drowning
1893

RM
121

Rhodes
Canyon

45m

RM
122

Rattlesnake
Canyon

Rock

25m

123.5

Amine
Canyon

RM
123

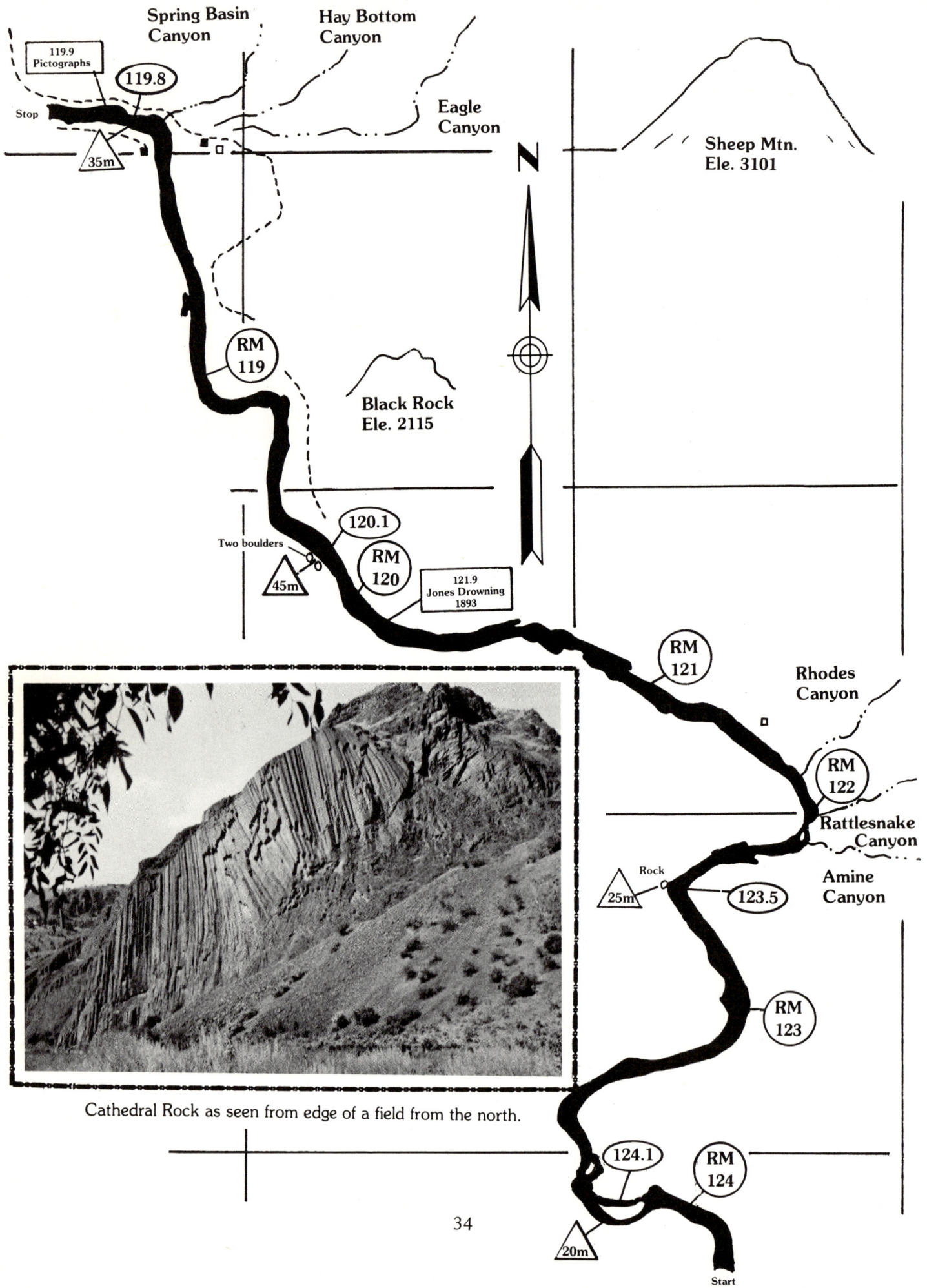

Cathedral Rock as seen from edge of a field from the north.

124.1

RM
124

20m

Start

DRIFT TIME

KAYAK	CANOE	DRIFT BOAT	RAFT	RIVER MILE
12m	13m	16m	20m	124.1
15m	17m	20m	25m	123.5
				121.9
28m	30m	36m	45m	120.1
21m	24m	28m	35m	119.8
				119.9

Across from this "U"–shaped bend, high on the right, can be seen the side of Coffin Rock. This fan–shaped formation, seen earlier, now appears to be feet sticking out of coffin. This area with beach is called Big Bend. There is good swimming here and a good camping area. There is, however, a shortage of firewood at this site due to frequent use. (Downstream about ¼ mile on left is a large flat area with lots of trees and good campsites.) Big Bend is about 12 miles above the Clarno Bridge.

Below Big Bend about 1 mile is another **Island Checkpoint**. (This is an island at high water only.) This is one of the few islands on the John Day with trees. A good beaching area can be found around the point on the downstream end of the island. The island has very good camping. 1 mile below the tree island is a round rock on the left side of the river. This is a **Landmark Checkpoint**. There is an island about ½ mile below the round rock. At the far end of the island to the right can be seen Amine Canyon which comes down to the John Day from the right. At low water a slough goes behind the island.

As you round the next bend, to the left on the right bank can be seen a sagebrush flat. Three canyons enter the river here in about ¼ mile from the right. The first one is Amine and just downstream is Rattlesnake. As you pass Rattlesnake Canyon the Jefferson County and Wasco County line runs down the ridge to the left. Rhodes Canyon enters downstream in about 1/10 mile.

Below Rhodes and Rattlesnake Canyons is a long, quiet stretch. Left bank has several nice picnic spots. Ahead downstream the high ground in the distance is Black Rock (another Black Rock is below Clarno). Directly upstream is Amine Peak.

This was the location of the drowning of a man named Hal Jones in 1893. His body was found 3 months later on a sandbar 1 mile below Clarno Rapids. Another man drowned looking for the body. Jones' young bride watched him drown but was unable to help him.

Just below the site of the Jones drowning, about ¼ mile, are two large boulders on the left bank. This is a **Landmark Checkpoint**. Downstream after a sharp left turn, can be seen a huge basalt formation. The author has named this Cathedral Rock. The river makes another sharp right turn at Cathedral Rock and proceeds straight for about ¾ mile.

A bluff with trees along its base and a ranch on the right is another **Landmark Checkpoint**. On the right above the road is an overhang in the cliff. Next to it is a notch with a juniper tree upon the top of the

35

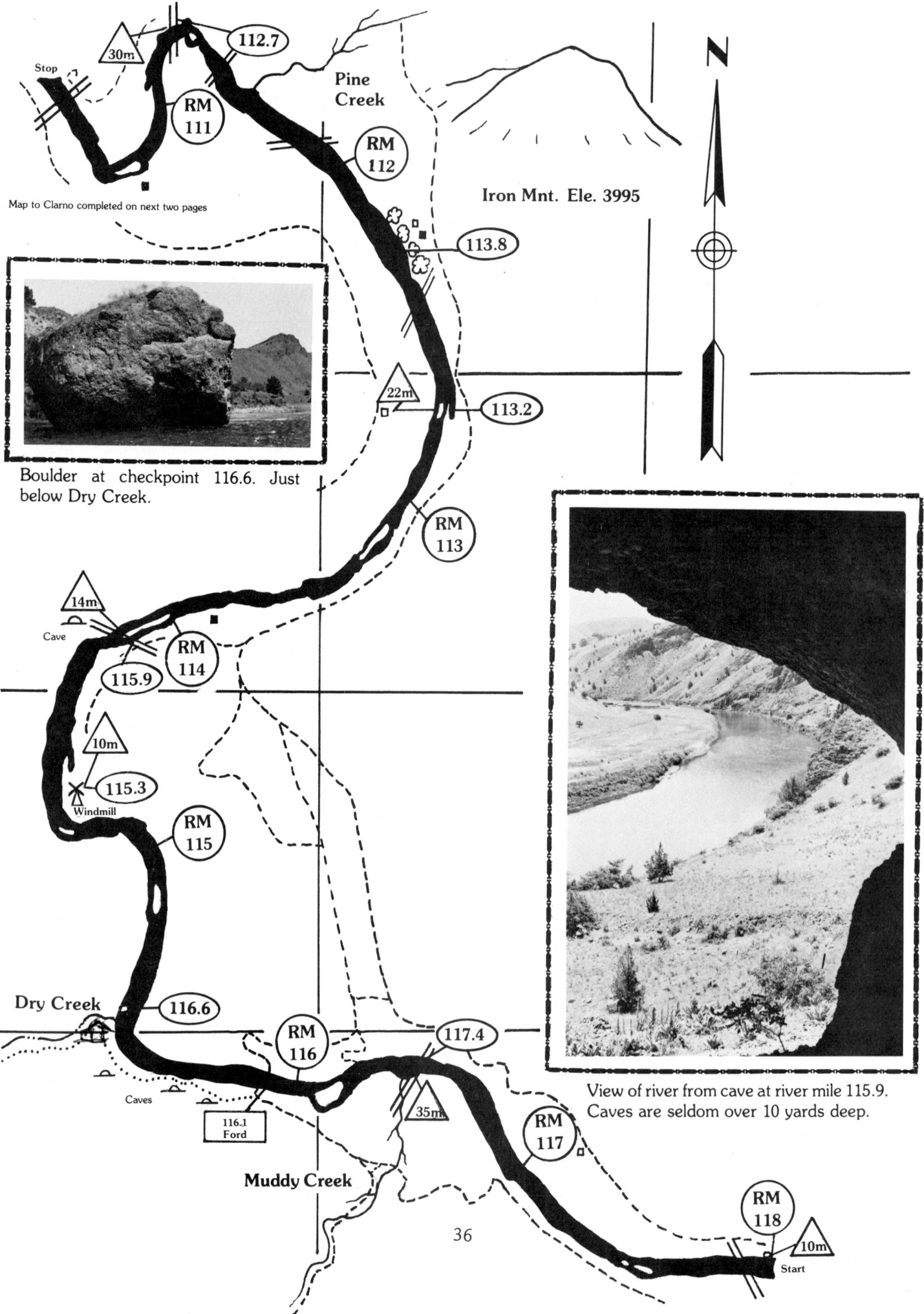

30m

Stop

112.7

RM
111

Pine
Creek

RM
112

Iron Mnt. Ele. 3995

113.8

N

Map to Clarno completed on next two pages

22m

113.2

Boulder at checkpoint 116.6. Just
below Dry Creek.

RM
113

14m

Cave

115.9

RM
114

10m

Windmill

115.3

RM
115

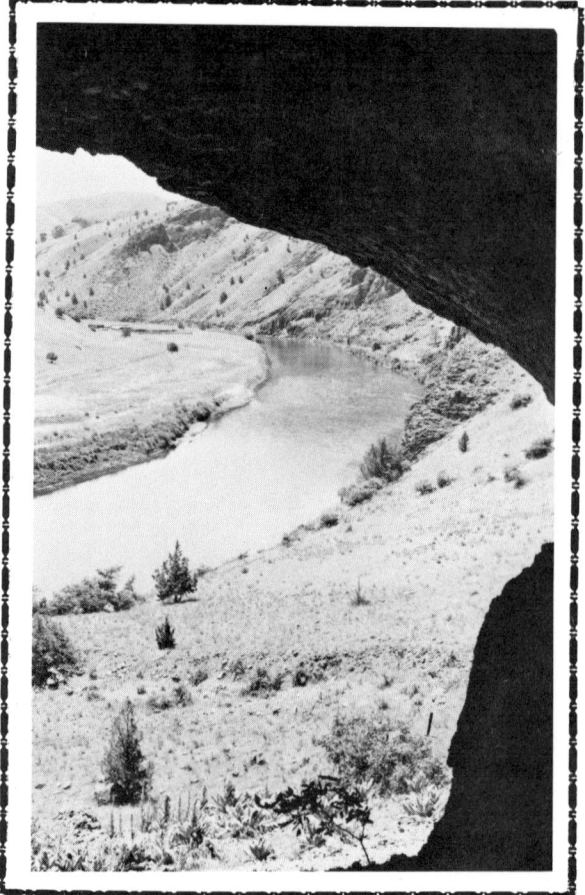

Dry Creek

116.6

RM
116

117.4

Caves

116.1
Ford

35m

Muddy Creek

RM
117

View of river from cave at river mile 115.9.
Caves are seldom over 10 yards deep.

36

RM
118

10m

Start

DRIFT TIME

KAYAK	CANOE	DRIFT BOAT	RAFT	RIVER MILE
6m	6m	8m	10m	
21m	24m	28m	35m	

bluff. You may note that the rocks have a red hue (under the overhang). These are some Indian pictographs possibly several hundred years old. If you see the road turn up the hill between two small bluffs, you've gone too far.

118 <u>Powerlines</u> cross the river here, a large boulder is on the right. The boulder is a **Landmark Checkpoint.** You are now 8 miles away from the Clarno Bridge. Water below here becomes very quiet and there may be some wind in the afternoon.

? Possible Take Out

118.4 The river sweeps to the right at medium water. You should see a bar. The left channel holds more water, but either should be O.K.

The canyon to the left holds what is known in the area as Muddy Creek. The creek runs into and out of Muddy Reservoir, about 3 miles up. All the land in the basin and a great deal of the land in the Clarno area is controlled by a large corporation. Locals know it as the Big Muddy Corporation, but it does change hands occasionally.

Up Muddy Creek to the west about 5 miles is Galligher Canyon, named for John Galligher, a pack train operator who was killed by Jim Berriway. Berriway, who was traveling with Galligher, hid the body and took the pack horse outfit to Canyon City. The body was found and Berriway was tried at the gold camp. He was found guilty and hanged in a new suit of clothes purchased by the miners. His skull is said to be on exhibit in the Canyon City Museum.

As you look up Big Muddy Canyon above some bluffs, the river flows around to the left behind some bluffs. One of the bluffs comes right down to the river.

117.4 Just below the bluff about 100 yards, the powerlines cross the river. This is a **Landmark Checkpoint.** Under the powerlines is an irrigation pump and a concrete platform. Rusty pipe is also nearby.

As you pass under the powerlines, you should see an island ahead. Both channels are possible depending upon the flow and height of the water. Island has a little elevation in the center and quite a bit of brush. Big Muddy Creek comes into the river above the island.

116.1 Here the river widens and two gravel bars are across from each other. Just above is a gravel bar which is sometimes an island. To the left is a depression in the bank and a large boulder about 3½ feet across. This marks a ford used when the river is lower.

After you pass the ford, there is a bluff on the left, and sloping ground going up to some large rocks. Ahead is

DRIFT TIME

KAYAK	CANOE	DRIFT BOAT	RAFT	RIVER MILE
11m	12m	14m	18m	116.6
				115
6m	6m	8m	10m	115.3
8m	9m	11m	14m	115.9
				114.1
13m	15m	17m	22m	113.2
				113.8
				112.1
18m	20m	24m	30m	112.5

(handwritten note in left margin: Camp 6/26/95 / Last Camp To / Clarno Bridge)

a dome structure with several caves. These caves, like all caves in this area, are very shallow.

On the left is Dry Creek. Below is a large boulder, the size of a small house. This is a **Landmark Checkpoint**.

In the distance the high ground is Iron Mountain. This will be the predominant high ground on the right for about 15 miles. It runs from Clarno to Butte Creek. The river makes a sharp turn to the left and at low water there will be a bar. A pyramid-shaped rock is straight ahead. Around the corner is a windmill.

The windmill on the right is a **Landmark Checkpoint**. As you drift below the windmill, the butte structure ahead on left has no name but is 2,441 feet in elevation.

Ahead can be seen a shallow cave; below to the right is some irrigation pump equipment and 16" irrigation pipe coming out of the river. Powerlines pass overhead. Powerlines are a **Landmark Checkpoint**.

There are dwellings and irrigation equipment on the right shore.

The island on the left can be seen when the water is low; at high water you will see willow trees protruding out of the water. To the left about 1/8 mile away is a small white shed on the hillside. This is an **Island Checkpoint**. Sometimes another island is visible below at medium water.

There is a large grove of trees on the right and power-lines above the trees. House in the trees may not be seen from the bank.

The powerlines cross again. Ahead is where Pine Creek enters the John Day.

A flash flood that came down this creek in 1935 was said to have had a crest 30 feet high. It swept every-thing away in its path; cattle, buildings, fences, etc. No life was lost but much damage occurred. The power-lines beyond the creek above the bend are a **Landmark Checkpoint**.

Charlie Hill worked at the Hilton place at the mouth of Pine Creek. About 1882, Charlie hired a Chinese cook out of The Dalles. He had several over the years and got along with them well. Somehow this new one took offense to something Charlie had said or done and acted strange for a day or two. One evening as Charlie was taking some air on his front porch, the Chinaman came out with a freshly brewed cup of

38

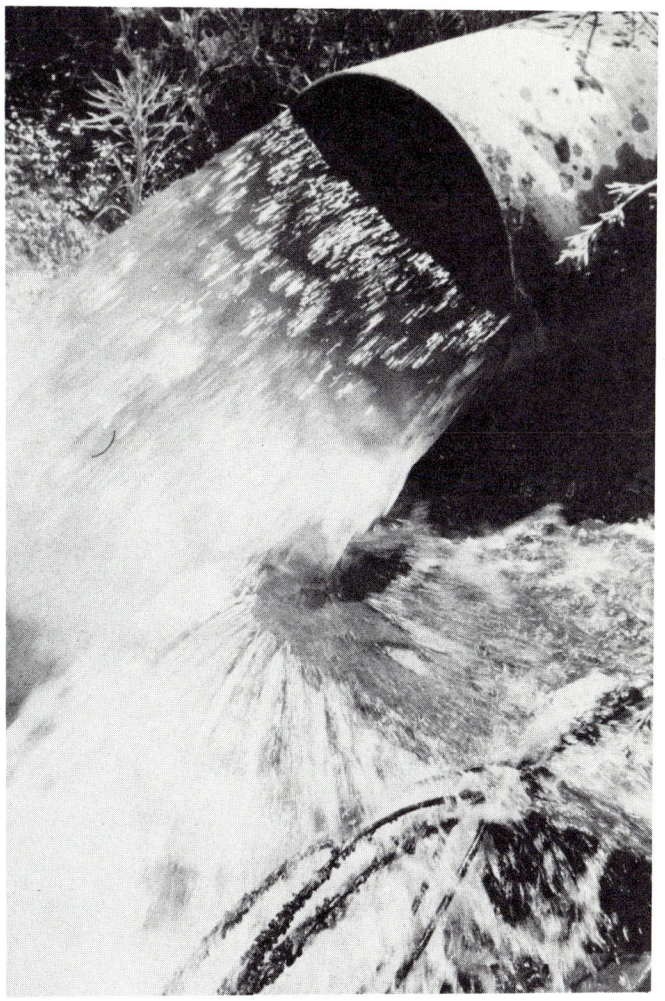

Top left: Boater enjoying the scenic beauty of the John Day. Right: Water, the life's blood of agriculture along the river; many irrigation pumps and pipes from the past and present can be seen along the banks. Below: The Clarno Bridge from just upstream, deep water on other side of gravel bar — a favorite mooring place of the riverboat, John Day Queen. Bluffs on right — site of a double drowning in 1916.

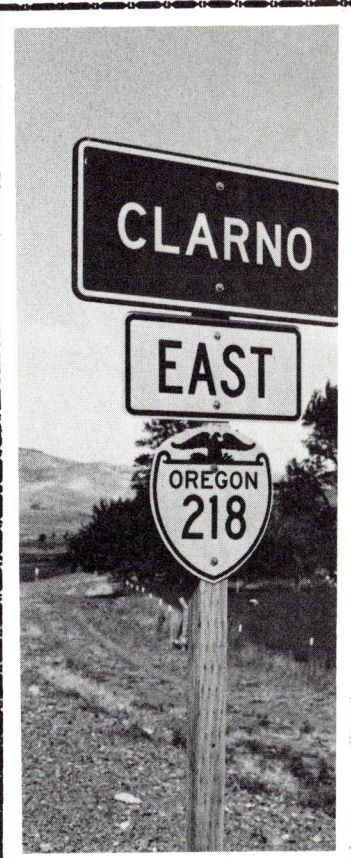

39

KAYAK	CANOE	DRIFT BOAT	RAFT	RIVER MILE

coffee and gave it to Charlie. Charlie got suspicious and said he didn't want any. The cook insisted and said "you drinkie" and Charlie got more suspicious. Charlie didn't say anything, he just got up and got his .44 caliber pistol, loaded it and went back to the porch. He laid the pistol down, pointing it at the Chinaman, with the hammer cocked. He told the cook "you drinkie it yourself," he argued. Charlie pointed the pistol at him and said "you drinkie or I'll blow your damned head off." The Chinaman drank it down and went inside. Nothing happened right away but later that night, the Chinaman got violently ill and died.

Charlie, being quite a few miles from town, decided he'd better take the dead cook to the sheriff. He loaded the body in a buckboard and drove off. The road was poor in those days and the hills and valleys were steep. Charlie said every time he went up the hill the corpse would slide to the back of the buckboard, but when he went down hill the body would slide down under the seat and would be looking up at him. Charlie got him to town okay, but he said that every time he was offered coffee "he could see that dead Chinaman's face." He never touched another cup the rest of his life.

As early as 1914, geologists felt that this area might produce oil. A prospect well was drilled east of here about 2 miles in November of 1927. The Clarno Basin Oil Co. was formed and sold shares for $10.00 each. Sunday afternoons saw local investors patiently waiting for the geyser that never came. Some oil and gas was found but not in paying quantities. The well went to over 4,500 feet deep and $300,000 was invested in the project. Some intermittent drilling continued until 1939.

112.8 The river makes a sharp turn to the left and a structure can be seen with irrigation equipment. Nearby structure has concrete base and wood top.

112.9 A dwelling is on the bank down river straight ahead, island in front of dwelling. Black Rock is high ground in the distance. Johnny Clarno, a young man of 19, once watched a battle between the Warm Springs Indians and the Snakes from this prominent point about 1869. He said the Warm Springs Tribe routed the Snakes.

111.5 Powerlines cross the river here. Ahead, down river, can be seen the Clarno School.

110.1 An island can be seen on the bend as the river turns towards school house. Island has about 10 feet in elevation. Take either channel. Old pumphouse on left as river turns right. Behind school is lean-to-type barn.

40

Above: The McDonald Ranch. Laura McDonald was the youngest Clarno girl, born in 1867, the year her father and mother settled in Oregon. This was her home across the river from the Clarno homestead. Black Rock can be seen in the far distance. Below right: Laura's organ which was once said to have been installed on the John Day Queen about 1893 for dances and moonlight cruises. Below: The Clarno School built in 1914 by a carpenter from Antelope. Older school was below bridge on the left bank above the Carno homestead. The school is now on private land. Note the extra windows on the north side — a good educational practice of its day.

The John Day Queen I: In 1896 moored at the bar just above the Clarno Bridge. Built in 1892, the Queen was a pleasure craft 50 feet long by 10 feet high. It ran at high water only between the Clarno Rapids and up river some 10 miles. Charlie Clarno, its builder, sits in the doorway; his father, Andrew; mother, Eleanor and sister, Laura, on the bow are in the same picture. This boat was washed downstream in a flood about 1899 and was destroyed. It was rebuilt in 1905. (See page 44-45)

Left: Andrew Clarno (1820-1907). Photographs taken about 1870. Andrew brought his family in 1862 and settled on the homestead site about 1 mile downstream from the Clarno Bridge. Original house still stands made from hand sawed planks hauled by ox team from The Dalles. Right: Eleanor Clarno (1823-1897). Eleanor brought 8 children into the world; 6 survived her. During the Civil War journey to the West, she sewed several thousand dollars in gold coin into her petticoat. She was wearing this when their ship, the Ariel, was captured by the Confederate gunboat, Alabama, in December of 1862. Below: The Clarno Homestead as seen today.

43

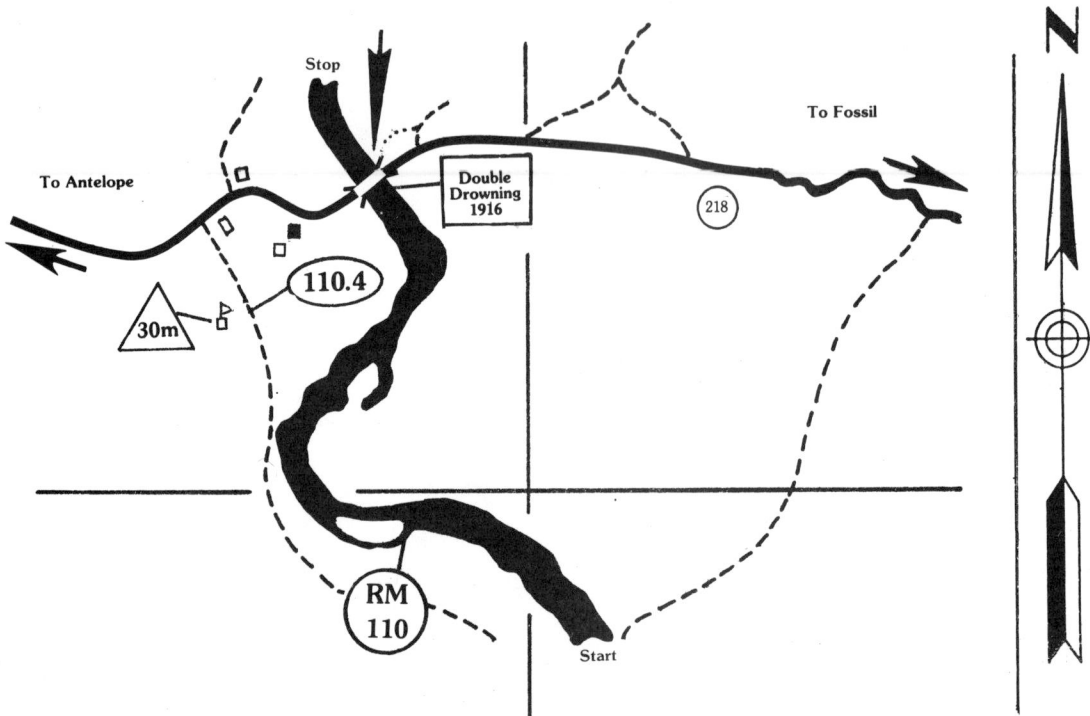

To Antelope

Stop

To Fossil

Double
Drowning
1916

218

110.4

30m

RM
110

Start

N

John Day Queen II in 1905, constructed after Queen I was destroyed in a flood. This craft was said to have better engineering than its predecessor. Parts from a steam threshing machine and machinery from a mine furnished power. Charlie Clarno, the builder, is in a doorway; his brother, John, on bow. Man in center is thought to be a horse buyer from Seattle representing the Japanese Army. Japan and Russia were at war that year.

DRIFT TIME

KAYAK	CANOE	DRIFT BOAT	RAFT	RIVER MILE
18m	20m	24m	30m	110.4
				110.7
6m	6m	8m	10m	110.8

				TOTAL
BURNT RANCH RAPIDS TO CLARNO BRIDGE				**MILES**
4:18	4:44	5:40	7:06	22.9
				TOTAL
TWICKENHAM TO CLARNO				**MILES**
6:48	7:29	8:55	11:14	33.2
				TOTAL
SERVICE CREEK TO CLARNO				**MILES**
9:24	9:35	12:16	15:30	46.2

Landmark Checkpoint—The Clarno School on left was built by W. D. Walker in 1913, from nearby Antelope, who built the school to replace an older school down river about ¾ mile. Note high windows on north side, a good educational practice for the day.

As you leave the school house at river mile 110.4, the river makes a sweep to the left towards the Clarno Bridge. High ground dead ahead is Iron Mountain, elevation at highest point is 3,995 feet.

Just before the bluff on the right is a sloping area, between the bluff and another rock outcropping. Directly across the river is a bar. This was the frequent docking place of the river boat John Day Queen—1892-1909.

A river steamboat built in 1892, the John Day Queen was 50 ft. long, 10 ft. high and 10 ft. wide. Built by Charlie Clarno who ran the ferry here about 1887, the paddle wheel steamer was sunk in May of 1909 while being lined down the Clarno Rapids 4 miles below the bridge. The steamer was used during high water (January to May) and is credited with saving much property and some lives during the 1894 flood. Andrew Clarno, his wife, Eleanor, and 5 children including Charlie came to this area from Bloomington, Ill. via New York, the Isthmus of Panama and California before settling here.

As you approach the bluff on the right, this is the site of the drowning of the Putnam brothers in 1916. At the end of the bluff upstream from the pumphouse is a leveled area. This is the east end of the old bridge approach which stood here from 1909 to 1973. As you pass under the bridge, this is a **Landmark Checkpoint**.

The Clarno Bridge was named for Andrew Clarno, pioneer stockman, who settled here with his family in 1867. Clarno's cattle were shipped to market as far away as Nevada and Utah. The present bridge was completed in 1973 and replaced the first bridge over the river here that was constructed in 1909. Clarno at one time had a hotel and a post office. A ferry ran under present bridge from 1886 to 1909.

45

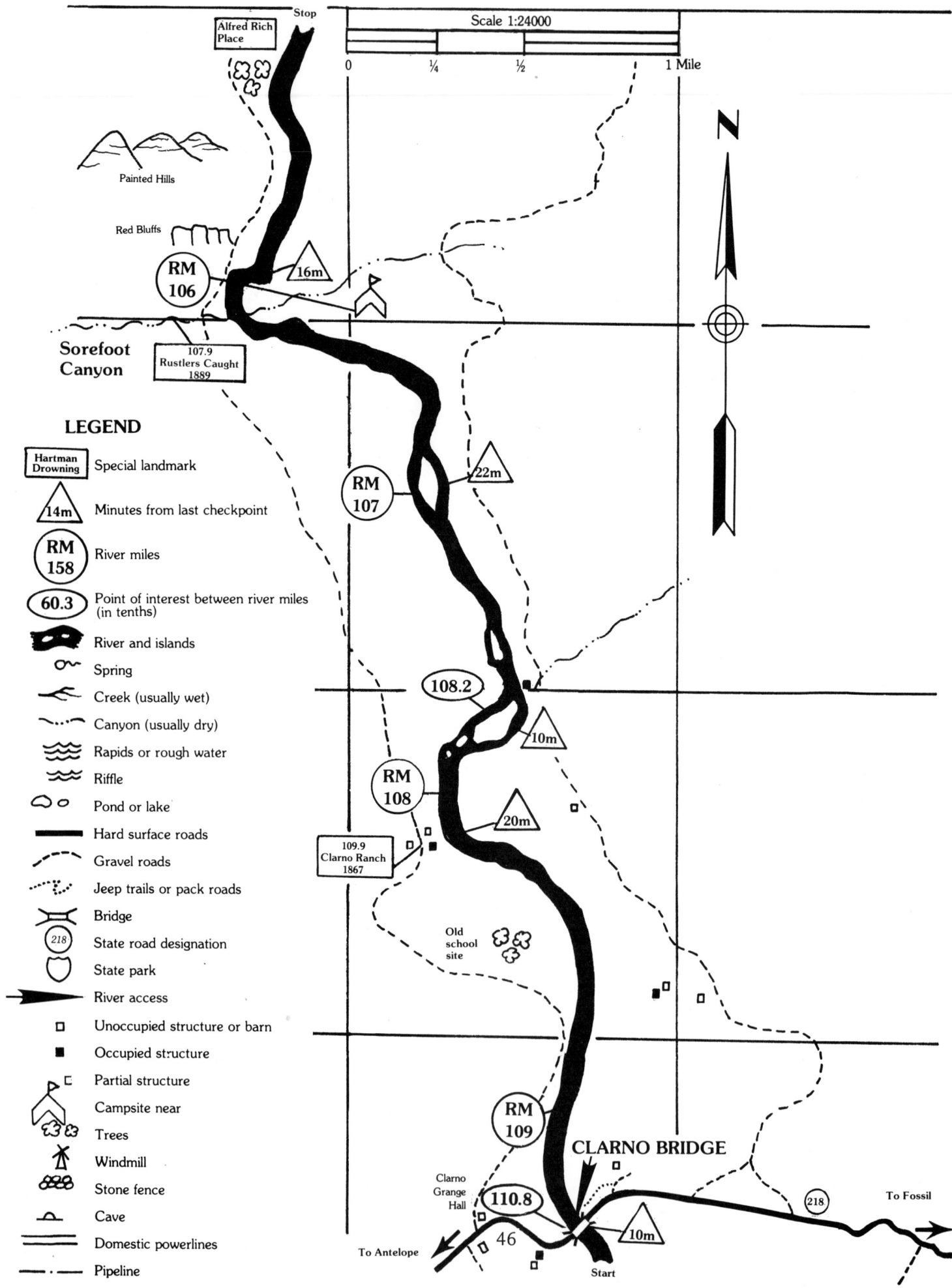

Stop

Alfred Rich
Place

Painted Hills

Red Bluffs

**RM
106**

16m

Scale 1:24000

0   ¼   ½   1 Mile

N

Sorefoot
Canyon

107.9
Rustlers Caught
1889

LEGEND

Hartman Drowning	Special landmark
14m	Minutes from last checkpoint
RM 158	River miles
60.3	Point of interest between river miles (in tenths)
	River and islands
	Spring
	Creek (usually wet)
	Canyon (usually dry)
	Rapids or rough water
	Riffle
	Pond or lake
	Hard surface roads
	Gravel roads
	Jeep trails or pack roads
	Bridge
218	State road designation
	State park
	River access
□	Unoccupied structure or barn
■	Occupied structure
	Partial structure
	Campsite near
	Trees
	Windmill
	Stone fence
	Cave
	Domestic powerlines
	Pipeline

**RM
107**

22m

108.2

10m

**RM
108**

20m

109.9
Clarno Ranch
1867

Old
school
site

**RM
109**

CLARNO BRIDGE

Clarno
Grange
Hall

110.8

To Antelope

46

Start

10m

218

To Fossil

CLARNO TO COTTONWOOD

River Mile: 110.8 to 40.2 (70.6 Miles)

	Estimated Drift Times	Recommended c.f.s.* 1400 to 4000
Raft	18 to 24 hrs.	Times to the left are estimates and reflect **time on water only.** More accurate times for this drift can be found on pages 57, 65, 79 and 86.
Drift Boat	15 to 19 hrs.	
Canoe	12 to 17 hrs.	
Kayak	10 to 15 hrs.	

DRIFT TIME

KAYAK	CANOE	DRIFT BOAT	RAFT	RIVER MILE	
				110.8	Clarno Bridge
				109.7	At river mile 109.7 on left is a low bar. This is believed to be the approximate final resting place of the John Day Queen.
				109.9	This is the original Clarno Homestead, site of the Andrew Clarno family. In its heyday the Clarno cattle were said to "have grazed over a thousand hills." During round-up as many as 15 cowboys were hired. The original house still stands, built in 1872 with lumber hauled from The Dalles by ox team.
12m	13m	16m	20m	109.9	On the left is the old Andrew Clarno Ranch which is a **Landmark Checkpoint.** High ground in the far distance is called Rattlesnake. Up river near a clump of trees stood the old Clarno School. You may wish to compare your drift time with the guide at this checkpoint.
5m	6m	8m	10m	108.3	As the river turns right there is an island. This island was once solid timber of willow trees and the locals used it for building purposes. Only a few trees remain today on the north end of the island. The center of the island is a **Landmark Checkpoint** at river mile 108.3. As you pass below the island there are buildings to the right along the river.
13m	15m	17m	22m	107	The island at river mile 107 is an **Island Checkpoint.** There is a low bar with some vegetation on the far end.
				107.9	To the left can be seen Sorefoot Canyon. This is the site of the first school in the area known as Rose Briar School. The building consisted of logs, dirt floor and a fireplace for heat. It was built around 1870.

Sorefoot Creek was named for a herd of rustled cattle found there about 1889. Rustlers stole the cattle some miles east of here. The cattle were driven a mile or so up the creek when the rustlers decided to hole-up and rest the sore-footed stock. The Sheriff and posse caught up with them there.

As you approach river mile 106, there are some red-colored bluffs to the left and some green painted hills.

*c.f.s.=cubic feet per second. See page 1 for details.

47

Above: Part of original Clarno corrals. With 350 head of cattle driven from California, the Clarno's built an empire. Below left: Charlie Clarno's tombstone. Right: The spark arrester from the John Day Queen, the only known surviving relic now in the Fossil Museum.

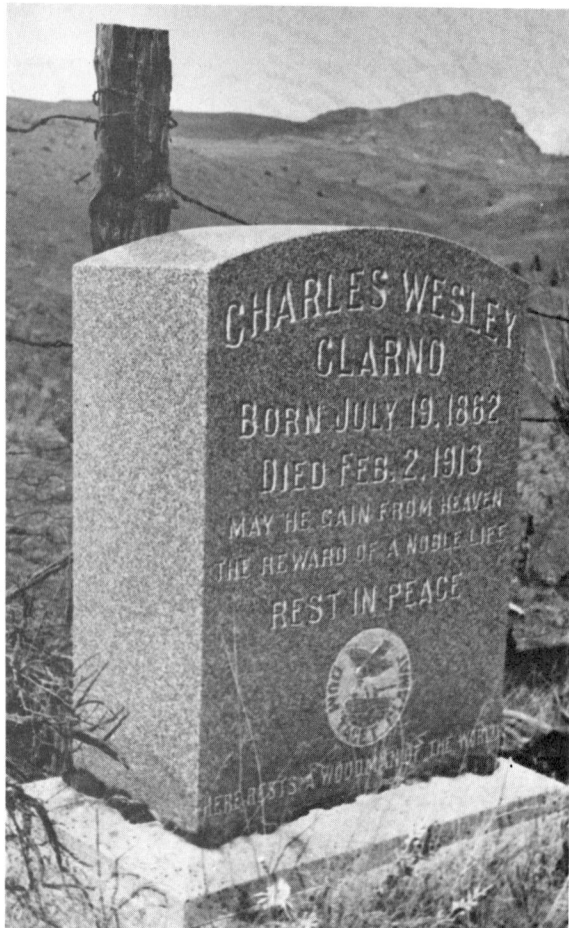

CHARLES WESLEY
CLARNO
BORN JULY 19, 1862
DIED FEB. 2, 1913
MAY HE GAIN FROM HEAVEN
THE REWARD OF A NOBLE LIFE
REST IN PEACE

48

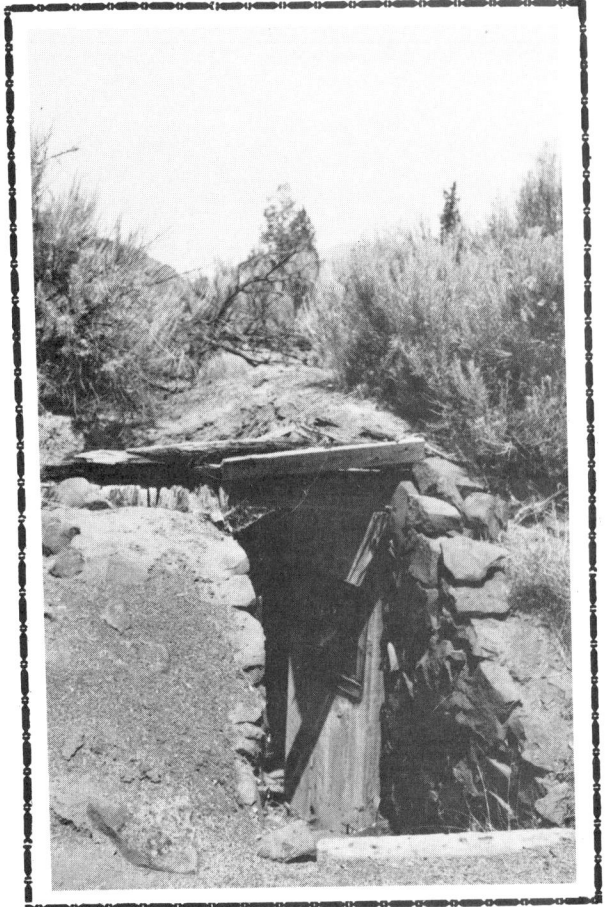

Above left: A 1923 Chevrolet engine used during the 30's for an irrigation scheme in Clarno area. Right: Caved in fruit cellar on the Alfred Rich place above the Clarno Rapids. Below: Wrecked canoe found in August of 1976 at river mile 105.9. Many boaters are deceived by the calm appearance of the John Day from its bridges and do not learn of its rapids and difficult water until it is too late. Fate of occupants is unknown. Old timers say, "If you take the river for granted, it will take you."

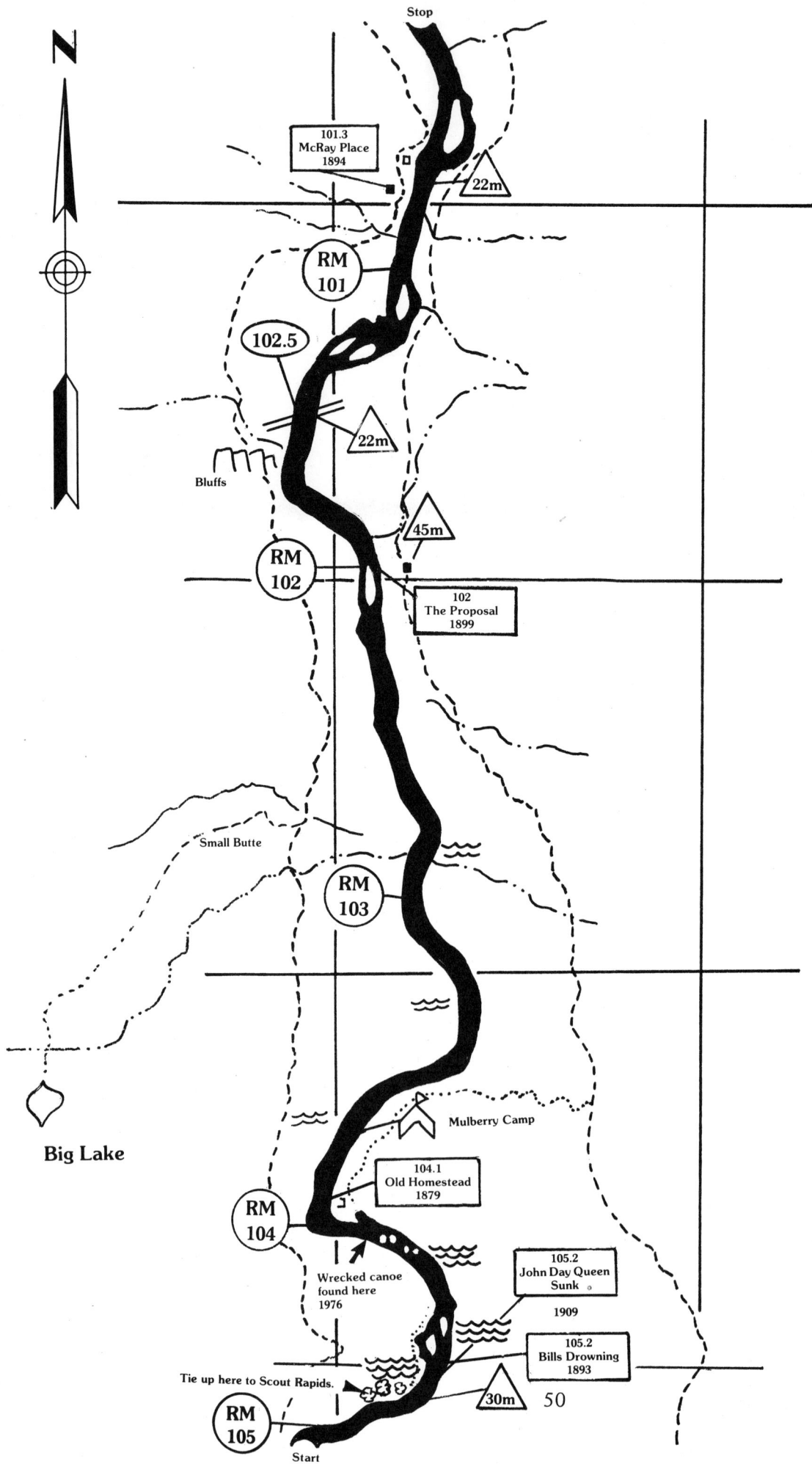

N

101.3
McRay Place
1894

22m

RM
101

102.5

22m

Bluffs

45m

RM
102

102
The Proposal
1899

Small Butte

RM
103

Mulberry Camp

Big Lake

104.1
Old Homestead
1879

RM
104

Wrecked canoe
found here
1976

105.2
John Day Queen
Sunk

1909

105.2
Bills Drowning
1893

Tie up here to Scout Rapids.

30m   50

RM
105

Start

Stop

DRIFT TIME

KAYAK	CANOE	DRIFT BOAT	RAFT	RIVER MILE
10m	11m	13m	16m	106
				106.3
18m	20m	24m	30m	105.2
				105.2

106 This is a **Landmark Checkpoint**. Clarno Rapids are about 1 mile from this location. Just below the red bluffs to the right and around a turn in the river is a very nice small beach.

106.3 Downstream from the bluffs and beach is a small riffle. The river sweeps left again and you are back in the quiet water. About 200 yards downstream from the riffle there are some trees concentrated on the left shore. In these trees is the site of an old homestead worked by Alfred Rich about the turn of the century.

The house is now gone, but the caved-in root cellar is still there. Other signs include a walled-off section near a small bluff which was some kind of enclosure for farm animals or chickens.

The river makes a sweep to the right about river mile 106. This is about ¼ mile from the Clarno Rapids. At 105.2 you will see some trees on the left bank. This is a good place to tie up and scout the rapids. This is a

105.2 **Landmark Checkpoint**. The Clarno Rapids vary between class II, III or IV depending upon the time of the year. There are numerous large rocks in the channel. Some can only be seen from below. To scout these rapids, tie up in the trees, walk across several hills until you can see where the river turns north. Work your way back along the river so you can see all obstacles, etc. There is a footpath which runs above the river for about 100 yds. below the trees.

About 300 yards into the rapids is a large boulder on the right shore. This is the approximate site of the sinking of the John Day Queen, in May of 1909.

105.2 Clarno Rapids. There have been some drownings here; a man named A. H. Bills drowned below the head of the rapids about 1/8 mile. Bills was looking for the body of Hal Jones in 1893. Bill's body was found in the Columbia River near The Dalles several weeks later, wearing only a shirt collar. The body was identified by a neighbor who was selling wool there.(Story on pg. 35).

In 1900, a ferryboat built near Twickenham was lined through the rapids with considerable effort. The ferry was used at the Ferry Canyon Crossing during high water until about 1920. The ferry was about 25 feet long and was built of 3" thick planks.

After you begin your drift through the Clarno Rapids, about a ½ mile downstream (the river keeps turning to

51

DRIFT TIME

KAYAK	CANOE	DRIFT BOAT	RAFT	RIVER MILE	
					the left), you will see several islands—one with a large and a small boulder. At medium high water, either channel is o.k. to take. Below the islands, you will find some very choppy water, lots of rocks, and some standing curls up to 3 feet high.
				104.1	As you leave the main section of rapids and drift into quieter water, Rattlesnake is still the high ground ahead and Iron Mountain is still on the right. To the right at river mile 104.1 is an old homestead in the trees above the blackberry bushes.
					This is thought to be the original Farquer McRay homestead before it was devastated by the 1894 flood. The flat ground below a rocky draw was once a cultivated field. This field now full of sagebrush is ringed by walnut, peach, plum, and mulberry trees. There is a good campsite at the far end of the field along the river. This is called Mulberry Camp. This is the last good camping and beaching area not on private land for 6½ miles until RM 97.5.
				103	As you drift past mile 103, to the left can be seen a small butte with some rock outcroppings on top.
				103.7	Here can be seen an irrigation pump and large framework. The first waterwheel in the area was installed near this site for irrigation purposes about 1895. About 1900 a gasoline engine was added. The wheel and apparatus was abandoned about 1906 when gasoline-powered pumps became popular.
28m	30m	36m	45m	102	The old Bills place built about 1889 is a **Landmark Checkpoint**. An amusing incident occurred here in 1889.
					Farquer McRay came to the Clarno Country with Zack Taylor Keys in 1876. Both men walked from The Dalles. Keys and McRay homesteaded in the area and worked hard to build up sizable spreads. Farquer was a large, raw-boned, black-headed Scotsman who spoke with a heavy brogue and vile tongue. It was said that he never had a bath in his life; and when he was found dead about 1935 in a creek, that he died under "mysterious circumstances" as he never had been that close to water before. Over the years he became a prosperous sheepman and was very honest, industrious and hard-working.
					Farquer had a house built down river several miles. It was quite elaborate for its day with 4 rooms downstairs and 2 upstairs. Many of the young ladies of the area knew he had his eye on some unlucky girl, but he never dropped a hint to any of them. Farquer continued to fuss over his house, doing the bedroom in a delicate pink and the parlor in apple green. The kitchen

53

DRIFT TIME

KAYAK	CANOE	DRIFT BOAT	RAFT	RIVER MILE
				102.4
				102.5
13m	15m	17m	22m	101.3

was all white and the upstairs in a bright blue. The house was completed during the winter of 1898, but the bride to be remained a mystery.

In June of 1899, Farquer had apparently chosen a young girl, Anna Bills, who was less than half his age. As she was bending over a well at the house above here, he put both arms around her and announced to her that she was his selection. The dumbfounded girl upon recovering her composure politely turned him down. Farquer tried to dissuade her from her "hasty" decision and pointed out that he had built the house for her and painted the rooms in colors she would like. (Anna was 14 and Farquer 35.) Farquer's courtship approach may have left much to be desired, but he certainly made up for wasted time once he saw his "bride to be" bent over the well that memorable day in June.

102.4 About a ½ mile past the Bills place are some bluffs on the left which come to the water's edge. The last one comes into the water farther than the rest.

102.5 Powerlines cross the river here. The river makes a sweep to the right, widens and goes by several islands. Directly downstream can be seen the old Farquer Mc-Ray Ranch, believed to have been built after the 1894 flood.

101.3 The Farquer McRay place, remodeled several times since 1900, is a **Landmark Checkpoint.** Below is an island.

One night in 1926 Mrs. Scott, Farquer's housekeeper, woke up in a cold sweat. She had had a nightmare where she kept seeing a gaunt-faced woman floating in the water, apparently dead. She described the dream to Farquer and her husband the next morning. They didn't think much about it until later that day when Farquer went down to the river a few yards from the house. Downstream was a small island and gravel bar. Something was floating near the island in shallow water. Farquer and Jim Scott went over to investigate. They found a partially-clothed body of a woman. The body was brought back to the bar and when Mrs. Scott saw it, she gasped, "That's the woman I saw in my nightmare." After fruitless efforts to identify the corpse, the woman was buried on the ranch in an unmarked grave. Her identity was never known.

James Scott and his wife worked for Farquer as foreman and housekeeper/cook. The Scotts had a daughter named Chrissy, who was about 5 years old. Farquer was devoted to her; he used to carry her around on his shoulders. Chrissy had golden hair and big blue eyes. In about 1930, Farquer came down with diptheria and

Right: Chrissy Scott's grave. Chrissy was 5 years old when she died, about 1930. Farquer McRay felt responsible for her death and constructed this enclosure himself. Grave stands about ¼ mile SW of the house below *(story on pages 54-56)*. Below left: One of the residents along the river who tends sheep and watches over the land. Life for some of these people is simple and trips to town average once per month. Roads are still very poor.

Below right: Site of the Farquer McRay house. Farquer built the original house for a 14 year old girl that turned down his marriage proposal in 1899; he never married. His legacy as a raw boned, foul mouthed Scottsman with a heart of gold is still remembered by old timers along the river.

55

KAYAK	CANOE	DRIFT BOAT	RAFT	RIVER MILE	

nearly died. One day shortly after he recovered he and Chrissy were playing in the John Day River near Farquer's cabin. Chrissy was in an old washtub and Farquer had tied a rope to one of the handles. He would push her out a ways and pull her back in. Chrissy managed to overturn the tub and fell into the cold water. Farquer got her to the bank, but as a result of the spill, Chrissy got very ill with a high fever, came down with diptheria and died.

Farquer never forgave himself; he insisted that she be buried on his ranch above the John Day. He tenderly constructed a special concrete wall 4 feet above the ground and placed a wrought iron gate at one end. Chrissy rests there to this day, protected in death by an enclosure which seems to symbolize Farquer's remorse. The gate is rusted shut and giant wild rye grass encloses the plot. After her death, Farquer moved to an upper ranch and never lived at the river ranch again.

Other stories persisted about Farquer that have become legends in the area. Once Farquer wanted to "fix up" before he took the stage to The Dalles. He went into the general store in Shaniko and asked to see new overalls. When he was shown a stock his size he said he needed a larger size; he bought them and slipped them over his old dirty ones and was on his way.

Once Farquer got drunk while visiting the Fenlyson place on North Pole Ridge. He crawled between clean sheets with his dirty clothes and muddy boots. The housekeeper was furious.

Farquer was a good man and well respected for his day. He paid his debts and helped his neighbors when they needed it. Many stories about old bachelors persist up and down the river, but all who lived along the John Day were accepted as friends and neighbors by those who knew them.

In February of 1887, a local man with a few drinks under his belt decided to slide down a loose gravely area on Iron Mountain. His toboggan was a large scoop shovel. Sitting in the wide metal part with his legs astride the handle, the descent began. As the hurtling missile picked up speed, the friction heated up the shovel scoop greatly, warming the posterior of the passenger. The journey ended in a patch of sagebrush. It was reported that the bottom of the shovel shown like new, but the passenger's bottom had seen better days! The speedy traveler had to take his meals in a standing position for some time.

99.3 Powerlines cross the river here and will cross again downstream.

56

DRIFT TIME

KAYAK	CANOE	DRIFT BOAT	RAFT	RIVER MILE
				99.5
21m	24m	38m	35m	98.1
18m	20m	24m	30m	98.6
				TOTAL
CLARNO TO BUTTE CREEK				MILES
2:25	2:42	3:10	4 hr.	12.2

99.5 High ground ahead is Horse Mountain. This mountain from this vantage point has a triangular head. The highest peak is 2,947 feet.

98.1 This point is where 12-inch irrigation pipe enters the river and powerlines recross. This is another **Landmark Checkpoint**. On the bank downstream to the right can be seen an old building. Farther downstream is a long barn structure. This is a sheep barn for the Butte Creek Land and Development Co. There are several large boulders in the water and on the left shore. Below there is a large square rock on the bank. The barn may be obscured by brush but it is 1/10 of a mile from the square rock. This is a **Landmark Checkpoint**.

98.6 In April of 1921, Ray Johnson, an employee of the Butte Creek Land and Development Co. (large sheep outfit), was found dead near here. A large pool of blood was nearby and a main artery was severed in his leg. The sheriff surmised that a sharp pair of sheep shears hanging from the saddle of his mule had somehow been rammed through his leg and he was unable to stop the bleeding.

In January of 1887, Jessie Ring and Park Doak were deer hunting on horses up on Iron Mountain when a large buck was sighted. Park shot and hit the buck in the nose. The deer bounded up the gully and stopped between them. Park couldn't fire for fear of hitting Jessie. When the deer lunged at Park and his horse, Ring threw a rope lasso and got the deer's horns. The buck then turned on Ring causing Ring's horse to spook, and headed down the ravine. Ring's horse fell, the deer fell, and did a double somersault, and Park shot the deer. Jessie was quoted as saying he "didn't like venison well enough to rope another."

On November 28, 1886, in Deep Canyon near here behind Iron Mountain, Henry Harvey was shot dead with 14 holes in him. The murderer of Roderick Grant earlier that month, Harvey holed up in Deep Creek after stealing a rifle and pistol near Mayville, overcoat and hat and saddle from another ranch on Butte Creek, and some spurs. When asked to surrender while camped under a juniper tree, he decided to shoot it out and several deputies opened up on him. Relatives declined anything to do with the bullet-ridden body, and he was buried in the Antelope Cemetery.

At about 97.5 there is a good, flat, large camping beach on the left.

57

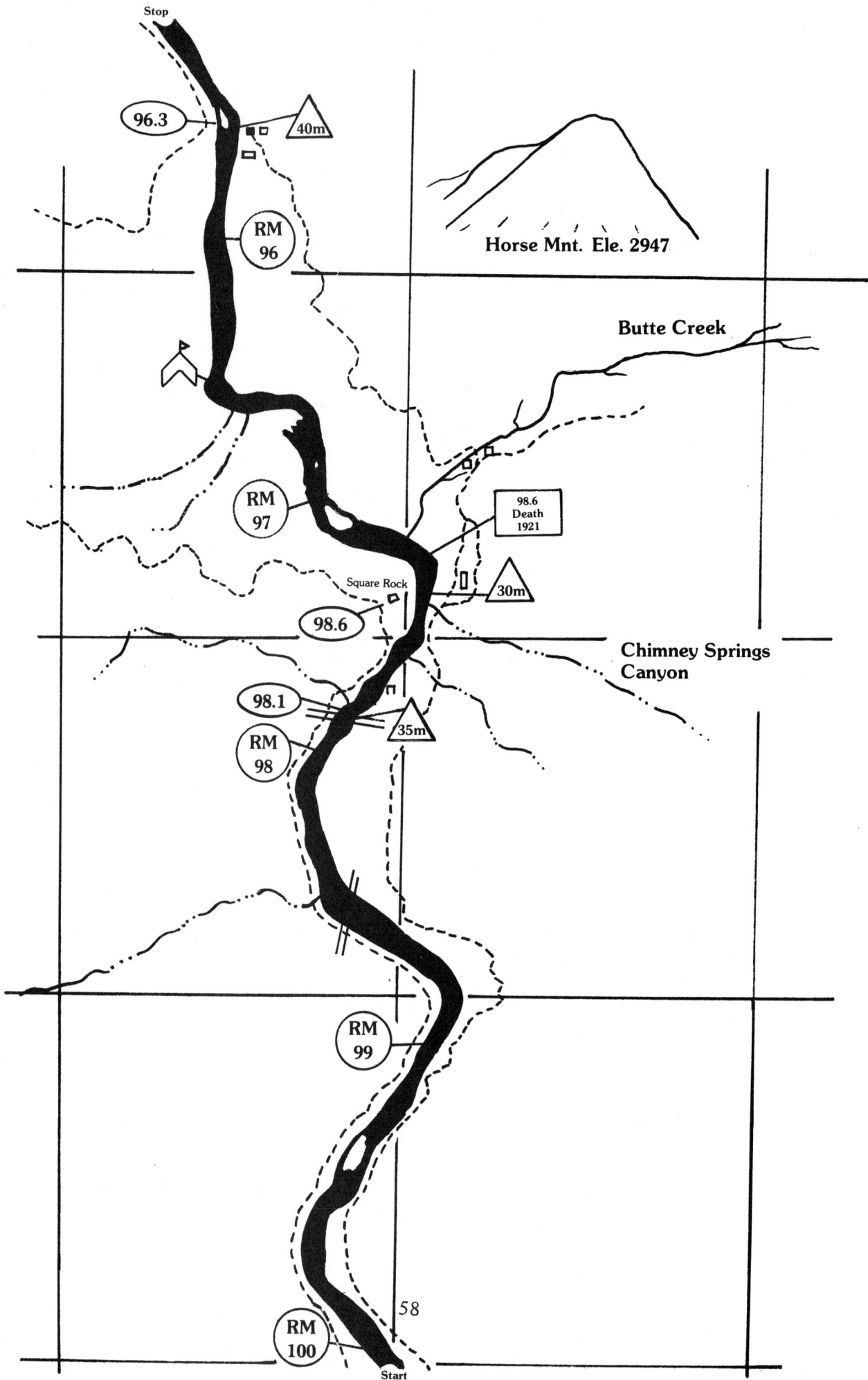

DRIFT TIME

KAYAK	CANOE	DRIFT BOAT	RAFT	RIVER MILE
				98.6
25m	27m	32m	40m	96.3
13m	15m	17m	22m	95.7
6m	6m	8m	10m	94.3

As you leave the barn at Butte Creek, the river makes a turn to the left. There is a big boulder on the left of the main channel. About ¾ mile below the sheep barn is a prominent outcropping of red rock that drops into the river. As you move down the river you are looking at the side of Horse Mountain. Visible about a mile away is a metal roof structure. This will be a checkpoint. Back upstream is the north end of Iron Mountain as it terminates in the Butte Creek Valley. High ground ahead on left is North Pole Ridge.

98.6 Chimney Springs Canyon comes in from your right off of Iron Mountain (look back).

In February of 1894, a man riding bareback approached a farmer working in a field east of here. He asked directions to the ford. The rancher directed him to it but cautioned him of the deep, swift water that time of year. The stranger seemed nervous and kept his horse between himself and the rancher, and also kept his hand near his face as if to keep from being recognized. The stranger said he "didn't give a damn about the high water," mounted his horse and proceeded to the river. He was lost from view as he went over a small rise. Several days later his horse was found grazing down river in a pasture. The fate of the nervous and apparently reckless stranger remains unknown.

96.3 At mile 96.3 is a **Landmark Checkpoint**, the buildings on the right previously mentioned.

It is believed that this is the site of the Butte Creek Bridge advocated by wool growers in 1897. Work was started in improving the road from Fossil and lumber was ordered for a temporary ferry until the bridge could be finished. The Dalles merchants who were needed to help finance the venture did not help as bridge backers had hoped. The venture failed.

At this point there are 3 rock formations entering the river. Opposite is an island.

95.7 Downstream a little ways, these rocks are a **Landmark Checkpoint**. Also right above the landmark checkpoint are 3 more rocks.

As you leave river mile 94, and pass a long island you will begin to drift to the northeast. The next 5 miles is known as The Narrows or the Great Basalt Canyon. At RM 94.6 a small bluff will protrude into the river. Just beyond the bluff about 100 yds. downstream is an excellent beach campsite. 200 yds. below this is another very fine beach camping area. This site is behind some large boulders on a sandy beach. On the left is Sherman Co. and on right is Gilliam Co. To the right is still Horse Mountain. Boulder in the left channel is a **Landmark Checkpoint** at mile 94.3.

DRIFT TIME

KAYAK	CANOE	DRIFT BOAT	RAFT	RIVER MILE	
				94.7	Beach campsite on sandy beach above river.
				94.8	Beach campsite behind boulders. For the next several miles there will be fairly fast water, rocks and minor rapids.
15m	17m	20m	25m	92.3	At mile 92.3 you will pass a large island with small trees and sagebrush. The center of this island is a **Landmark Checkpoint**. The river sweeps to the left and sharply back right again. The peaks to the right range from 1200 to 2000 feet in elevation.
				92.8	There is a good camping beach at this point on the bend.
9m	19m	12m	15m	91.6	As you pass river mile 91.6, there is a large boulder on the right bank. A very large flat surface faces upstream. This is a **Landmark Checkpoint**. Beyond the checkpoint rock are some high bluffs. You will see two very distinct arches about ½ mile apart. These are known as Arch Rocks. The elevation directly above the arches is 1200 feet. The rock formation is also called the Red Wall and is over a mile in length.
				90	Just below mile 90 there are two small islands, one in the right channel, one in the left. If you look up above the islands to the right you will see a jeep trail which terminates at the river's edge. The large island below will be an **Island Checkpoint**. This island is a large, diamond-shaped, bar with very little vegetation. Past the bluffs on the right are two nice beach areas. This checkpoint may be windy if passed in the afternoon.
11m	13m	15m	19m	90.5	
				89	At this point there are bluffs on the left, several rocks in the channel and several islands below here.
					In the spring of 1975 three canoes upset below here in very rough water. All but one man made it to shore and he became stranded upon a rock. Two men in the party hiked out for help while several stayed on the bank through the night. By morning a rescue boat was floated to the rock, and the man was taken off after a long, wet and cold night. That night some gear was recovered, but it was useless because it had not been packed in waterproof containers. All parties had life jackets in the boat, but they were not wearing them when the mishap occurred. The John Day can be hard on those who take it for granted.
				89.6	Pete Enyart Canyon enters from right.
				89.8	Big Gulch enters from the left here above small island.

60

N

Weathered latch on one of the many old buildings along the John Day.

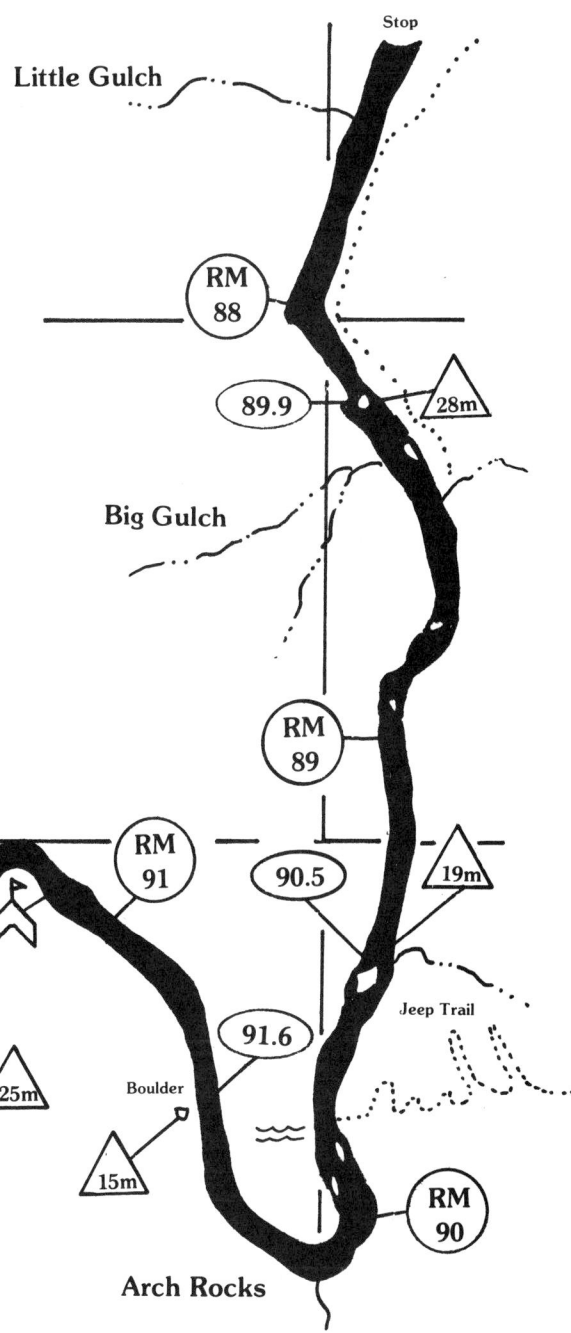

Little Gulch

Stop

RM 88

89.9

28m

Big Gulch

RM 89

RM 91

90.5

19m

92.3

RM 92

91.6

Jeep Trail

25m

Boulder

RM 93

15m

RM 90

Arch Rocks

Many farmers left the area years ago. Left behind are rusting relics.

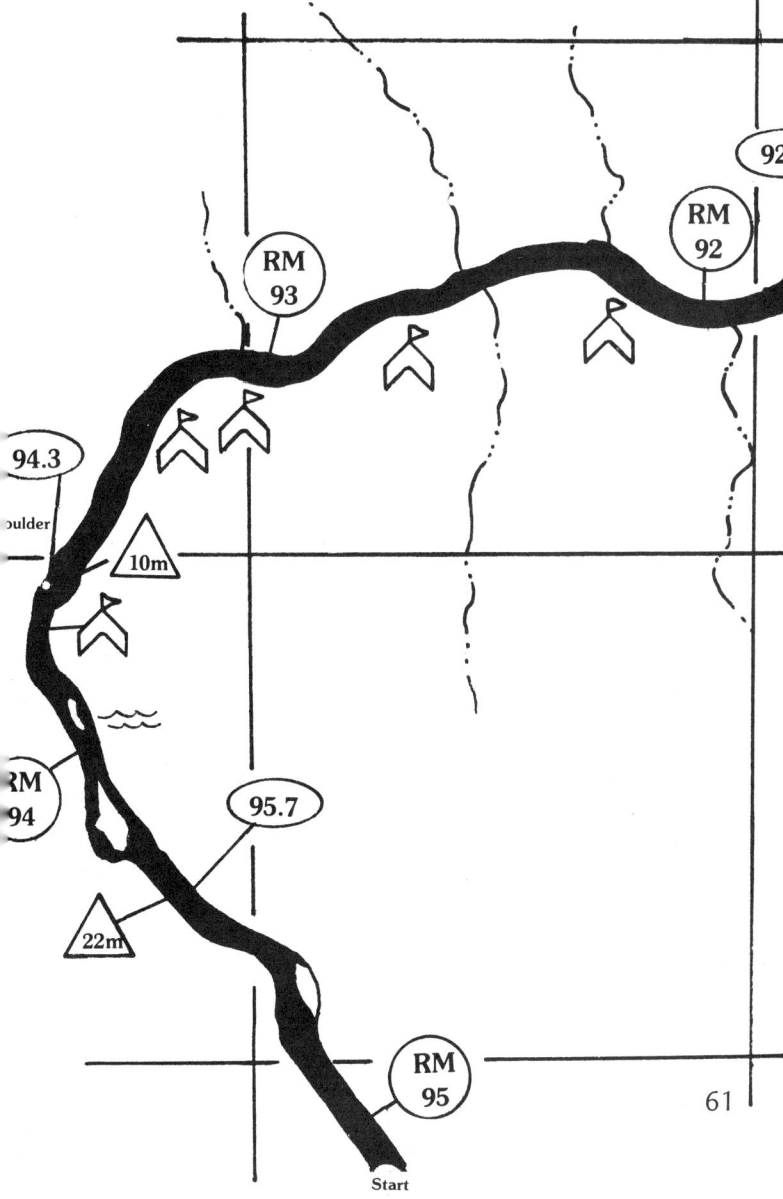

94.3

Boulder

10m

RM 94

95.7

22m

RM 95

Start

61

DRIFT TIME

KAYAK	CANOE	DRIFT BOAT	RAFT	RIVER MILE	
5m	6m	8m	10m	89.9	Just after you pass an island in the right channel, the river widens and narrows quickly. This is a **Landmark Checkpoint**. There is a bar island between the two bluffs.
				88.3	High upon a ridge to the right is a road built by the Corps of Engineers in 1960. The road was used to bring in equipment to obtain core samples for a feasibility study of a dam near 30 Mile Creek. This has been done at various spots along the river since 1916.
				87	Camping beach on left. Downstream big rocks.
				87.1	Two Islands.
				87.5	Here at the middle of the loop as the river turns left is Devils Canyon. High bluffs to right. Some eagles nest on these bluffs occasionally. Look for white stains on bluff.
20m	22m	26m	33m	86.4	As you come to mile 86.4, there are several large rocks in mid-channel—one smaller one on the right bank is leaning on another. This is a **Landmark Checkpoint** known as Leaning Rock. Thread your way through as best you can. The wind may be a factor here.
				86.6	There is a rock on the right bank with BM painted on it. This is a U.S. Geological Survey marking, and the elevation here above sea level is 1009 feet.
18m	20m	24m	30m	85	Here is a 12" irrigation line coming out of the water on the right bank. This is a **Landmark Checkpoint**.
				85.1	Zigzag Canyon enters from the left. This canyon comes off of North Pole Ridge.
				85.2	A pipeline crosses here. Built in 1963 it originates in British Columbia, Canada and runs to San Francisco.

The pipeline furnishes natural gas in the Bay Area. It was washed out one year later in December of 1964 by the Christmas flood, but was replaced again that same year. It is owned by Northwest Pacific Gas Transmission Co. It crosses under the river here and continues up Pine Hollow to the left.

In October of 1896, the J. W. Davis family lost two small children and 3 others were injured as the Davises were getting ready for church. They lived up 30 Mile Canyon and as Mrs. Davis was helping the children into the wagon, the horse spooked and ran, jolting Gracie, 7 and Oliver, 2, killing them instantly. Three other children were thrown but survived the accident.

Stop

RM
81

N

RM
82

RM
83

84.1

18m

RM
84

85.2
Pipeline
Crossing

Pine Hollow

30m

RM
85

Zig Zag
Canyon

86.4

33m

RM
86

RM
87

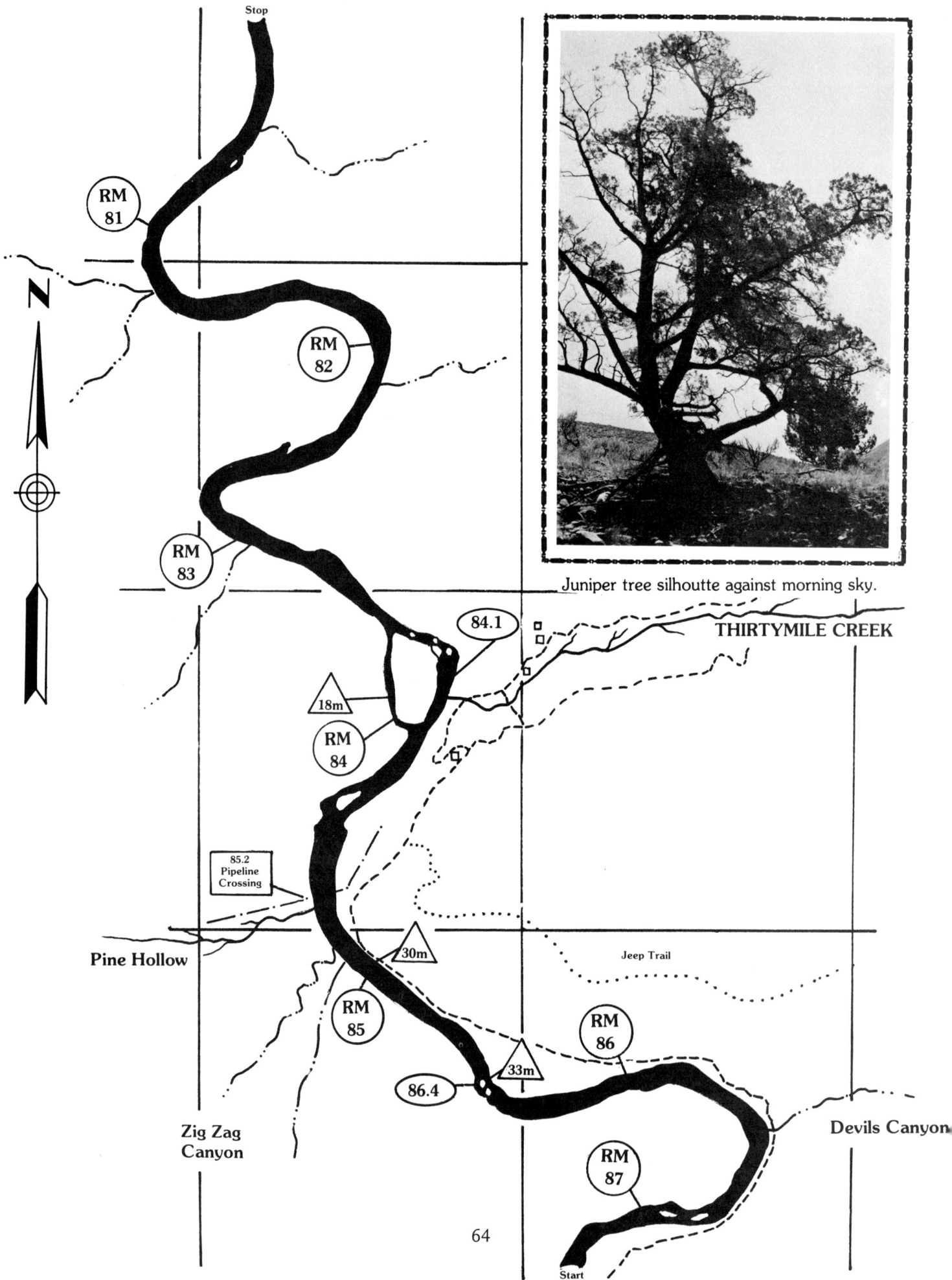

Juniper tree silhoutte against morning sky.

THIRTYMILE CREEK

Jeep Trail

Devils Canyon

Start

64

DRIFT TIME

KAYAK	CANOE	DRIFT BOAT	RAFT	RIVER MILE
11m	12m	14m	18m	84.1
				TOTAL
BUTTE CREEK TO 30 MILE CREEK				MILES
2:11	2:33	2:52	3:44	14.5
				TOTAL
CLARNO TO 30 MILE CREEK				MILES
4:36	5:15	6:02	7:44	26.7
30m	33m	39m	48m	80
				80.6
				80.7
				78

In 1908 an unfortunate hawk hunter, age 12, was found in 30 Mile Creek east of here several miles. The boy had apparently fallen from a high tree into a shallow creek and was knocked unconscious. By some chance a rider happened by who got off his horse to tighten his cinch. He heard the boy moan and found him beyond the brush with a fractured skull. The boy, Lester Frizzell, eventually recovered.

84.1 30 Mile Creek enters from the right at this **Landmark Checkpoint.** As you pass this checkpoint below there are several boulders in mid-channel. Pick your own way depending upon water height. To the left is a large bar island. Take right channel. It is believed that 30 Mile Creek got its name because its headwaters are about 30 miles from its mouth.

It seems that a number of young men were cutting juniper fence posts up the creek in January of 1897 and were playing poker at night. The legal tender consisted of money, posts cut and other items. One young man bet his money, his watch and all his fence posts at the gaming table. He also thought he held sufficient cards to bet his new Sunday britches. He was called and lost. The winner refused to loan the man's pants back to him, and at last reports he rode home in his long johns with the flap "flapping gracefully in the keen winter breeze."

Beef Hollow on your right at river mile 80. This checkpoint can best be determined by a large black rock on the right with sharp protrusions. The rock is about 8 feet across and is a **Landmark Checkpoint.** Beef Hollow comes in from the right.

80.6 The river sweeps left against the bluff. Stay right. Just beyond mile 79 you will find a good beach campsite on the left.

Beef Hollow which comes down from Crazy Hollow, got its name when two brothers named Armstrong were caught butchering a stolen beef about 1900.

80.7 Crazy Hollow, 1 mile above here on the right, got its name from a sheep herder who went crazy there about 1914. He ran to a nearby ranch and told the owner that a bunch of "toughs" were after him and he needed a place to hide. The rancher put him up in a bunkhouse for a few days until the sheriff came for him.

78 Whistle Point—This landmark above here on the ridge to the right started out as Cottage View Farm. A youngster came to the farm one day about 1915 when the wind was whistling around and nicknamed it Whistle Point. The Cottage View Farm name has faded but the name Whistle Point remains.

65

Buckskin
Canyon

Jeep Trail

N

Stop

73.3
Petroglyphs

Potlatch Canyon

73.3

1:05

RM
73

73
Stillwells
Ferry

Jeep
Trail

RM
74

HORSESHOE
BEND

The Saddle

RM
76

RM
75

77.8
Old Wagons
1928

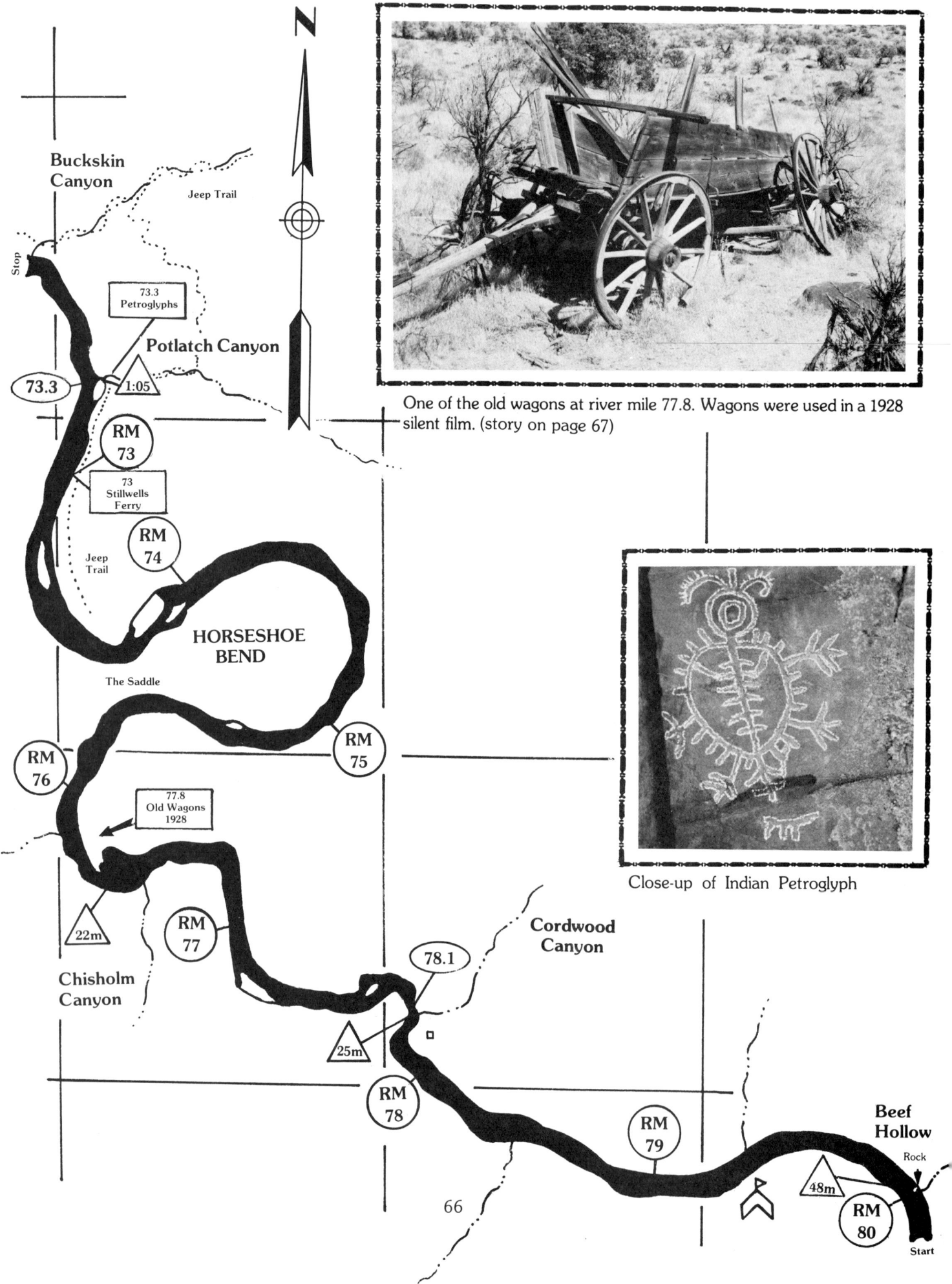

One of the old wagons at river mile 77.8. Wagons were used in a 1928 silent film. (story on page 67)

Close-up of Indian Petroglyph

22m

Chisholm
Canyon

RM
77

78.1

Cordwood
Canyon

25m

RM
78

RM
79

Beef
Hollow

Rock

48m

RM
80

Start

66

DRIFT TIME

KAYAK	CANOE	DRIFT BOAT	RAFT	RIVER MILE
15m	17m	20m	25m	78.1
				78.2
				77.6
17m	19m	17m	22m	77.8

As you pass river mile 78, look directly to your right above the trees on the bank. Here you will see an old sheep herder's cabin used about the turn of the century until about 1928. Around the bend across from the bluffs is a camping area and beach boat inlet. This is a **Landmark Checkpoint**. (Use the edge of the bluff for reference.) The canyon above is Cordwood Canyon.

This canyon got its name from some cordwood that was cut and stacked there for a number of years. It seems that about 1893 two brothers cut the wood for sale downriver. It is not known if the deal fell through or why it was left there, but the local ranchers used it for fencing and firewood until about 1920.

Just as you leave the checkpoint, there are some bluffs dead ahead. Markings indicate another party passed through here in 1946 (surplus rubber rafts available about that time). The other marking is an elevation checkpoint which puts you now 912 feet above sea level.

Chisholm Canyon enters from the left.

At river mile 77.8, the river begins to widen considerably. It will appear to bulge on your map. To your right are some basalt rock formations. Beach here if you want to see the old wagons which are located about 100 yards from here. They are near several juniper trees, above the beach and gravel bar on the right. The edge of the bluff will be a **Landmark Checkpoint**.

The old wagons have quite a story behind them. In the fall of 1928 a film maker who called himself Denver Dixon came up from Hollywood and filmed the Condon Rodeo that year. He got to talking with some of the locals and they decided to make a western silent film.

The story has it that he went back to the hotel that night and wrote the script. Later that fall he came back and made the film. He used all local actors except for himself and his wife whom he called Art and Delores Mix (the Mix name was big in those days). The plot was simple, about 3 cowboys saving a wagon train from Indian attack. These wagons were used in that film, and were made at the Sid Seale and Nelson ranches some years before. They were covered with muslin to look like covered wagons. The wagons were brought off a high hill east and a little south of here, and the film makers took hand-cranked shots of the wagons coming down the 40° to 45° slope. Other scenes were shot at river mile 76.9.

Often the term "flying wheels" is used as a figure of speech, but some of these wagon wheels actually flew

67

				DRIFT TIME	

<table>
<tr><th>KAYAK</th><th>CANOE</th><th>DRIFT BOAT</th><th>RAFT</th><th>RIVER MILE</th></tr>
<tr><td></td><td></td><td></td><td></td><td>76</td></tr>
<tr><td></td><td></td><td></td><td></td><td>76.2</td></tr>
<tr><td></td><td></td><td></td><td></td><td>73</td></tr>
</table>

all the way to Oklahoma and back. The iron tires around the old wagon wheels have become collector's items. You see them with or without the wooden spokes in yards, patios and other spots of interest in various landscaping schemes. It seems that in June of 1976 the Bureau of Land Management contracted a private helicopter to fly two BLM men on a fire rehabilitation survey over the Rock Creek area. Flying over the John Day, the pilot saw the wagons and landed as he wanted to make some part of a pot-bellied stove with the wheel rims. The 3 iron tires were strapped on to a tool-hauling plate below the helicopter, and were eventually taken back to Oklahoma.

Some locals interested in the river and the historic value of the wagons, along with the BLM District Manager, became involved in getting the rims returned. A letter was written to the helicopter pilot by the BLM. The rims were eventually returned, and the BLM employees received mild rebukes for their roles in the affair. All is forgiven now that the tires are back near the wagons where they belong. Please leave all wagon parts in place for others to enjoy. They will look much better here than in your garage or patio.

76 As you leave river mile 76, the river makes a sweep to the right. At this point you are beginning to enter Horseshoe Bend. First line of bluffs are 1000 feet high, the highest reach 2400 feet. The next checkpoint will be 40 minutes to an hour away when you get to Potlatch Canyon.

76.2 As you enter the horseshoe, you will notice a low point to the left. This saddle, which is only about 100 yards wide, separates the river. It will take about 40 minutes to completely drift around the horseshoe. Down river on the left is a low flat island; take the right channel. Below the island about 75 yards, look up on a ledge and you will see a nest possibly belonging to an osprey.

73 Behind a double fence post, with a support in the middle, is part of an old cable-tightening apparatus which was used by a man named Stillwell from about 1895 to the 1920's.

Stillwell had gone to town one day around 1906 and had left his small boat ferry on the Gilliam Co. side. When he returned, the boat was on the other side of the river. Someone had used it going the other direction. Stillwell started to cross the cable hand-over-hand. He was an epileptic and had a slight seizure about half way across. His muscles contracted and his grip tightened on the cable. He was reported to have

68

DRIFT TIME

KAYAK	CANOE	DRIFT BOAT	RAFT	RIVER MILE
40m	44m	52m	1:05	73.3
				73.7
				72.2
				72.7
				72.9
				71.1
16m	18m	21m	27m	71.6

told friends, "I guess I just hung there and shook until it passed over." Stillwell continued his journey across the cable.

Stillwell farmed the flat above here to the right about 1898. He decided to try his hand at watermelons one spring. He got the ground tilled, seeds planted and waited. That year it was hot and the watermelons grew so fast that they rotted before he could get a road improved enough to get them out by wagon. Stillwell told a local rancher, "it seems a feller could walk for miles on those rotten melons."

73.3 As you drift along to the right you will see a cliff with a road running along the base. Where the concave cliff meets the road at the corner are Indian petroglyphs. As you pass this point, prepare to put in at a beach and grassy area about 75 yards below. The edge of the cliff is a **Landmark Checkpoint**. Potlatch is an Indian name meaning big feast. Petroglyphs* are probably religious symbols. This was a sacred place to the Indians. Look, take pictures, but otherwise leave them alone.

73.7 On the right at river mile 73.7 Buckskin Canyon enters the John Day. A jeep trail also comes down this canyon.

72.2 On the right is a good beach campsite.

72.7 Beach Campsite on right.

72.9 There are two springs coming out of the hillside. The water should be good if you get it from its source. Cattle contaminate the water above the bank. Strips of green vegetation mark the springs.

71.1 At this point a basalt formation ends abruptly.

71.6 Here can be seen a large island. This is an **Island Checkpoint**. Above the island can be seen a jeep trail to the left. Just below the island on the right is a spot called Cave Bluff. Here below the island about ¼ mile, is a small cave which goes back under the bluff, and there is sometimes a rocky beach inside. If you plan to go in stay close to the bluff as you leave the island. The cave is about 10 yards deep and 15 yards wide. Here is a good place to take pictures, especially of other boats passing. Wild geese sometimes use the cave for shelter.

About 2 miles above here stands a 12 room house that never became a home, at least for the Blakely family. Mark Blakely of Portland bought a nearby ranch. He planned to bring his family here in the summer. In 1918 he had a huge house constructed with indoor plumbing, full basement, upper and lower screened-in porches and a reservoir that was as big as a good-sized swim-

*Petroglyphs are actually carved with flint into the rock and painted. Pictographs are painted only.

Below left: Indian petroglyphs. Petroglyphs are actually carved into the rock and color added. Pictrographs are Indian markings that are painted only. Many canyons and caves along the John Day and tributary creeks have Indian markings. Exact interpretation is unknown but Indians camped and fished near here.

Above left: View from one of the old shacks found along the river. Right: part of the cable tightening apparatus for Stillwells Ferry at river mile 73. Stillwell once had a bumper crop of watermellons growing here, but the road was too poor to get them to market. Below right: A view of two rafts drifting in the morning sun. Some of the cliffs and palisades tower over 3,000 ft. from the river.

Above: A circa 1920 Ford truck cab sunning itself above here in a pasture. There are numerous types of vehicle bodies, farm machines and old wheat combines that are just left to the elements after serving the ranchers for years. Right: Rafters at Hoot Owl Rock enjoy the view. Below: the old Blakely place — a 12 room house that was never lived in. Huge for its day (built in 1918), its owner went broke before he could move his family from Portland to occupy it. (Story on pages 69-73). Many much smaller empty houses dot the landscape. They were once proud homesteads where children were born and loved ones died. Many are now just storage sheds and cattle shelters.

Stop

RM
66

△ 27m

67.6

Stair Step
Palisades

RM
67

△ 30m

Bull Basin

RM
68

Fern Hollow

69
Murder
1927

RM
69

Jeep Trail

△ 27m

RM
71

RM
70

Cave Bluff

71.6

Two
Springs

Jeep
Trail

RM
72

Start

N

72

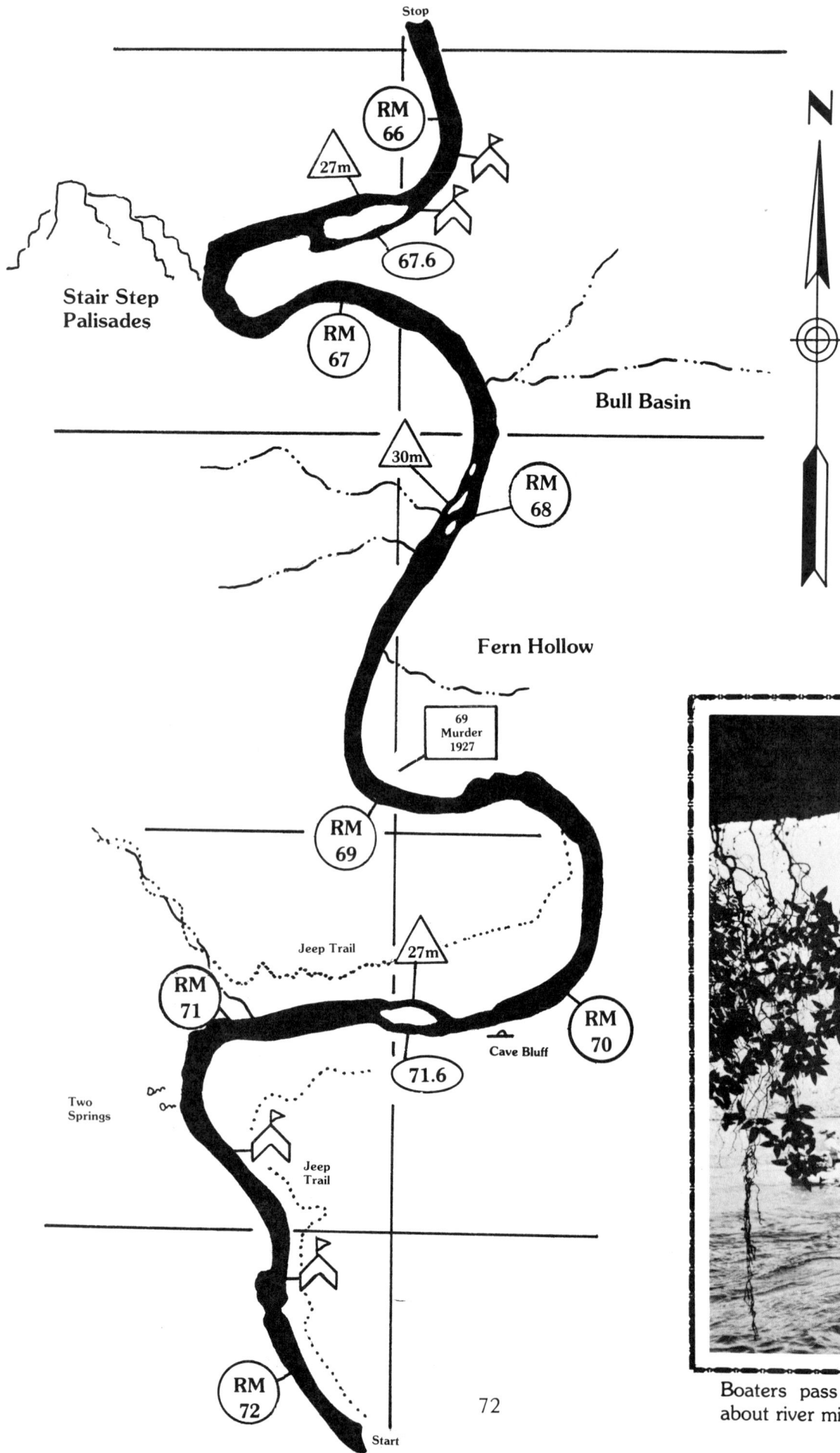

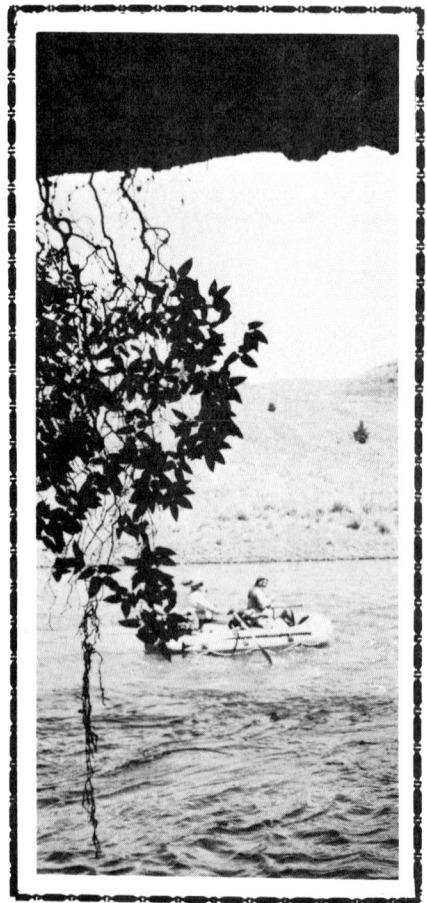

Boaters pass by Cave Bluff
about river mile 71.8.

DRIFT TIME

KAYAK	CANOE	DRIFT BOAT	RAFT	RIVER MILE
				70.7
				69
				69.2
18m	20m	24m	30m	68
				67.2

ming pool. He lost his money in a recession about 1920 and had to sell the property. Blakely was heard to say in a Condon bar as his fortune was slipping away, "if I could raise 5 or 6 hundred thousand dollars, I'd pay half my debts and tell the rest to go to hell." Over the years the house and grounds have been a sheep camp, and the basement is now a cattle shelter. Some families did occasionally rent the place, but could not afford to furnish it. The house now sits alone surrounded by wheat fields and the long forgotten dreams of the Blakely family.

70.7 As you leave the protection of the bluffs at river mile 70.7, you may encounter some wind. Several times the author has drifted through here when it has been windy.

69 Above here on the right in December of 1927, a bizarre event took place. Ray Ferguson, despondent over a marriage proposal rejection, killed his girl friend, Viola Richmond. While driving Viola and a girl friend home one evening, he stopped his car and attacked both girls with a hammer. When the hammer broke, he pursued the terrified girls through a wheat stubble field with his Chrysler touring car. He stopped his car and started firing at the girls with a shotgun. While they were both begging for their lives, he blew the top of his girl friend's head off, at point blank range. Her companion fled and although wounded, managed to escape.

A heavily armed posse of over 40 men with bloodhounds searched for Ferguson. The next day his car was found stopped by a rock near the rim of a canyon where he had apparently tried to run it off the evening before. The fugitive was tracked down the John Day several miles to Cow Canyon where the posse and dogs lost his trail. Several days later a little girl traveling to her friend, Viola's, funeral in Condon, led searchers to his body found in the Richmond Schoolhouse. Ferguson had returned to within several hundred yards of the murder scene and had committed suicide with the shotgun. His hat was found blown across the room and there was blood spattered on the walls of the school which was named for the family of the girl he had loved and murdered.

69.2 To the right is Fern Hollow and the high ground ahead is called Bull Basin.

At this point there are several islands depending upon the water height. The second island is an **Island Checkpoint**. Beyond the checkpoint to the left is a high butte-like structure with an outcropping of rock on top.

67.2 The river makes a sharp turn to the right and above to

N

Stop

58.6

RM
58

30m

Lon Eakin
Flatt

Cow Canyon

RM
59

Citadel Rock

60.1
Hoot Owl Rock

32m

RM
60

Grass Canyon

RM
61

Jack Knife Creek

23m

Double
Drowning
1922

62.7

RM
62

Shell Rock
Canyon

RM
63

RM
65

65.9

25m

RM
64

Pearson
Canyon

Long Hollow

74

Start

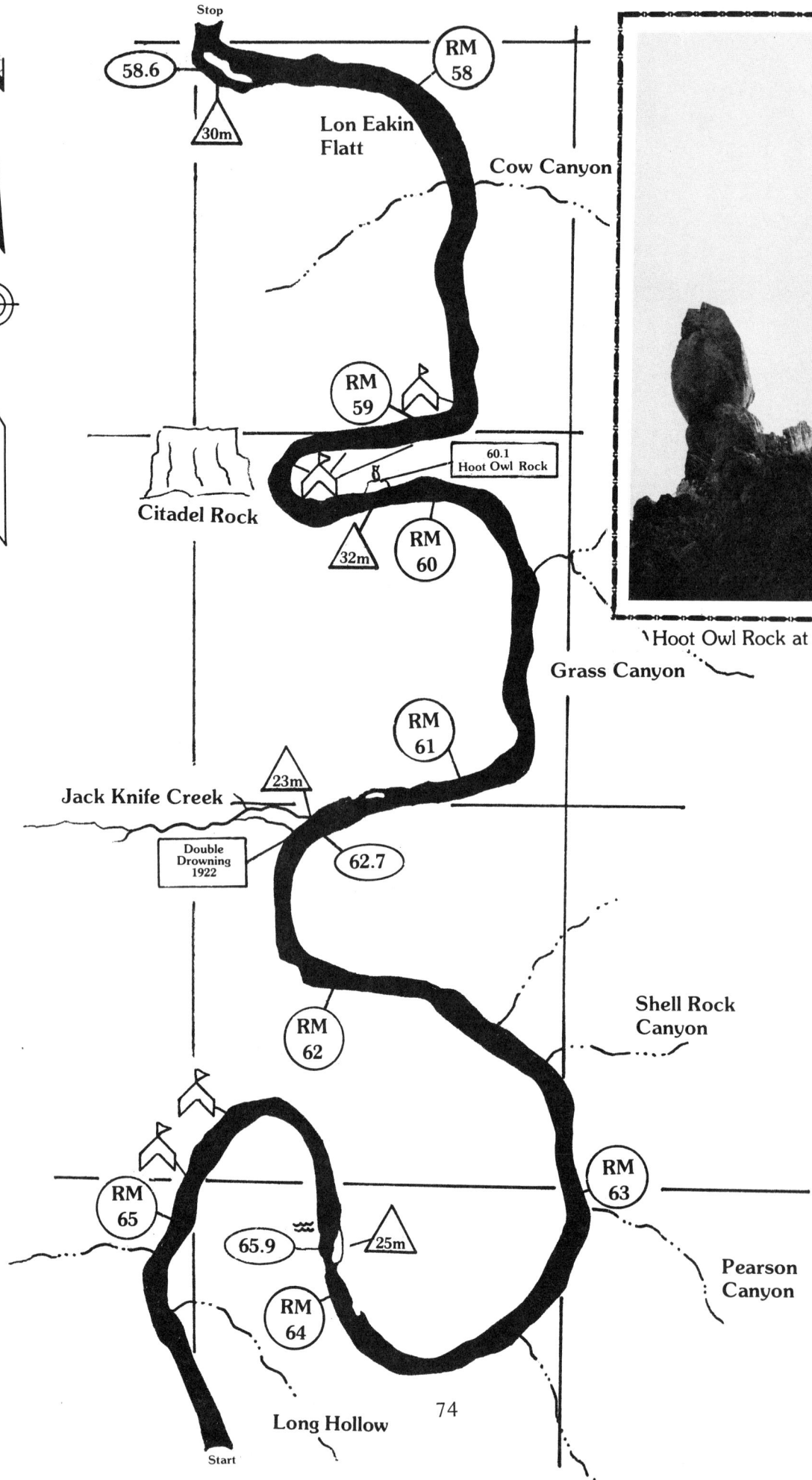

Hoot Owl Rock at river mile 60.1.

DRIFT TIME

KAYAK	CANOE	DRIFT BOAT	RAFT	RIVER MILE	
16m	18m	21m	27m	67.6	
15m	17m	20m	25m	65.9	
12m	19m	15m	23m	62.6	

the left can be seen a spectacular ½ mile of stair step palisades. This formation is the east end of a larger series of hills and mountains called Adobe Point. Downstream to the right are more palisades which are part of the northwest end of Bull Basin.

67.4 — As you look to the left around mile 67.4, you will see a large, long slide which goes from the top to the bottom of the palisades. As you approach the next island you will note that it is one of the few islands with any elevation. This is an **Island Checkpoint**. Take the left channel.

67.7 — At the end of the island is a beach campsite, and two more can be seen on the right downstream.

66.8 — Long Hollow comes in from the right.

65 — From mile 65 and 65.3 are some beach campsites on the left bank.

You will find the next checkpoint at river mile 65.9. This is an **Island Checkpoint**. There may not be water behind the island except early in the drifting season. Good riffle and standing waves can be seen opposite the island.

64.5 — As you go around this horseshoe-like section of the river, the high ground ahead is Wilson's Point. Entering the river from the right at river mile 63 is Pearson Canyon.

63.4 — Shell Rock Canyon enters from the right.

Jackknife Canyon is on the left with lots of vegetation. Use the creek in the center for **Landmark Checkpoint**. The vegetation goes back about ¾ of a mile. Just downstream from the creek entrance there is a long low bar island which is usually visible.

A man named O'Sullivan homesteaded at the head of this canyon. He was reported to be a railroad man in Canada who came home once a year to impregnate his wife and leave a little money. Two daughters drowned near the mouth of Jackknife Creek while crossing on horses around 1922. One girl was pinned against a rock by the current. While the other tried to save her both died. A son was killed about the same time, when lightning struck an outhouse. A short time later the rock cabin homestead was abandoned. A story has it that during the prohibition days some men from Seattle used it for a still. Grain and materials were flown in and the whiskey was flown out.

61.7 — Grass Canyon enters from the right.

61.9 — There are some large boulders in the channel here; be on the alert, be careful.

75

DRIFT TIME

KAYAK	CANOE	DRIFT BOAT	RAFT	RIVER MILE	
					East of here about 4 miles is Indian Springs, site of an Indian war between Snake River and Columbia River Indians in 1850.
				60	As you round the bend to the left you will see a round barrel-shaped rock high to your right. This is called
20m	22m	26m	32m	60.1	Hoot Owl Rock. This is a **Landmark Checkpoint**.
				60.5	As you are in the middle of the hairpin turn below Hoot Owl Rock, to your right is a very large round palisade. This has been named Citadel Rock for its resemblance to similarly shaped European forts. There are some nice camping areas to your right on the flat, and there is one small beach campsite downstream at the end of the bluffs to the left. The water is quiet and deep there.
				59.7	At this point Cow Canyon comes in to the John Day Valley from the right. The fugitive, Ray Ferguson, was tracked by a posse with bloodhounds to the head of this canyon in 1927. Story on page 73.
				59.9	As you begin to see the land flatten out on the left into a large sagebrush area, this is Lon Eakin Flat, named for an early homesteader who farmed here in the early 1900's.
18m	20m	24m	30m	58.6	At the end of Lon Eakin Flat is a low long island. This will be an **Island Checkpoint**.
				57.2	Piano Box Canyon enters right. Nat Wheat Canyon comes from left.
					Piano Box Canyon got its name from a cabin put there for a sheepherder about 1915. When asked how he liked his new quarters, he answered, "t'aint much bigger than a piano box." Name remains to this day.
				57.9	At this point on the left side of the river is another government elevation reference point — TB16J painted on a rock. You are now 693 feet above sea level.

Fisherman's Note: Until the early seventies only suckers, squawfish, carp, bullfish and steelhead populated the river. The steelhead runs were sporatic in the fall and winter months. Smallmouth bass were introduced in 1971 and quickly spread up and down the river. Bass fishing is better when the water clears up in June. Fish for the bass near rocky banks and weeds. Also, fish in deep holes and at the base of the rapids and riffles.

Joe Peters' body was found under the snow above here in 1939. Peters, a sheepherder, was missed from a sheep camp when he failed to return and two of his three dogs came back to camp. The other dog led searchers to the body. No foul play was suspected.

KAYAK	CANOE	DRIFT BOAT	RAFT	RIVER MILE
21m	24m	28m	35m	56.6
				55.3
18m	20m	24m	30m	54.3

The sheepherder's lot was far from picturesque in his eyes. A poem by Diego Veranos says it below:

> On John Day breaks so high and steep
> Full many a day I've herded sheep;
> I've herded sheep up on those breaks,
> And killed the lively rattlesnakes.
> But woe is me, those days are gone,
> And all my sheepherding is done,
> And well I wish myself away
> From Oregon and the John Day.
> No more along these breaks I'll creep
> With frozen fingers herding sheep;
> For this hard winter and deep snow
> Has formed in me a desire to go
> To warmer climates far away
> From Oregon and the John Day.
> Just now I wish I'd never come
> Or left a warmer, better home
> Like many thousands more have done
> To make a raise in Oregon.
> If I can make enough in time,
> To take me out of this cold clime,
> You bet your life I'll stomp away
> From Oregon and the John Day.

What Diego Veranos lacked in poetic skills he made up in his dislike for sheepherding on the John Day.

56.6 Ahead on the left is a **Landmark Checkpoint**. This is where Little Ferry Canyon enters the John Day. Below this checkpoint are two flat islands (about 200 yds. downstream). One is on the left and one is on the right. Look upstream from this point. The hills on the left and also on the right are part of a larger mountain called Indian Cove.

55.3 As you pass Little Ferry Canyon at river mile 55.3, there are some red bluffs on the left. Just over these bluffs is the river again about ¼ mile away. This is called the Gooseneck.

As you enter the canyon area there are some prominent red bluffs on the right. Where these bluffs end is a small beach area. This is a **Landmark Checkpoint**. There is a great deal of history in this canyon and some interesting sights, but camping is poor due to cattle, fences and general vermin ascending from the marsh on both sides of the creek.

54.3 The George Owens place is to your right across a creek, a marshy area and up the road about ¼ mile. There is a windmill and a stone corral near the cabin. There is a gate through the fence near the trees ahead. Down

77

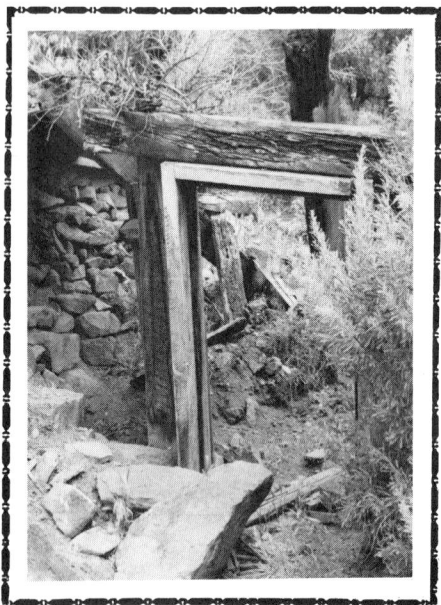

Stop

RM
51

52.1

RM
52

⟨15m⟩

RM
53

Charlie's
Place

Bert's
Place

□   ♀ Spring

Owens Basin

Jeep
Trail
♀
Spring

George's
Place

□   ✗   🪨🪨🪨 Stone Corral
Windmill

THE GOOSENECK   ⟨35m⟩

54.3

Ferry Canyon

RM
55

RM
54

Large squaw fish caught just below Little Ferry Canyon.

Little Ferry Canyon

⟨35m⟩

56.6

Indian Cove

RM
56

57.9
Death
1935

**Nat Wheat
Canyon**

RM
57

**Piano Box
Canyon**

78

Start

DRIFT TIME

KAYAK	CANOE	DRIFT BOAT	RAFT	RIVER MILE
				TOTAL
30 MILE CREEK TO FERRY CANYON				MILES
3:56	4:34	5:09	6:33	29.8
				TOTAL
BUTTE CREEK TO FERRY CANYON				MILES
6:15	7:07	8 hrs.	10:17	44.3
				TOTAL
CLARNO TO FERRY CANYON				MILES
8:22	9:09	11:10	14 hrs.	56.5

river is the Charlie Owens place along the bluff about a mile away. Bert Owens lived over the hill about 2 miles away.

If you get out to explore, remember to wear boots as there are rattlesnakes here, especially around the old structures where the rodents hide. If you are interested in some history, the easiest way is to stay in the boat and read the following:

Ferry Canyon was named for a ferry that ran across here from about 1893 to 1920. Part of the cable–tightening apparatus can be seen on the left bank. An old combine drum held the cable the ferry crossed on. On the right bank are the remains of the George Owens homestead and a rock corral used to hold livestock. Around the homestead can be seen wooden water pipes which George used to irrigate some alfalfa. The tongue and groove pipe, made of cedar, was originally part of the Condon water system and was brought here about 1903.

There were three Owens brothers living near the canyon: Bert, George and Charlie. Charlie's place is on the right about ¾ of a mile below.

Many colorful stories spring up about old bachelors whose sanitary habits usually left something to be desired. It seems that Charlie had a guest for supper one day and the visitor asked if his plate was clean. Charlie told him that it was as clean as soap 'n water could get it. Towards the end of the meal, Charlie placed his plate on the floor of the cabin and called his old hound dog to clean up the scraps. The visitor asked the dog's name. Charlie replied, "ole Soap 'n Water."

Bert was said to have tried to rescue a lamb that had fallen on a ledge somewhere above here. He had himself lowered to the ledge by a rope. When he reached the ledge, he found the lamb was fine, but a large rattlesnake was between him and the lamb. What did he do? He took off his boot, attached the lace firmly to the bottom eyes and beat the snake off the ledge by swinging the boot by the laces.

It was said that the Owens brothers made good whiskey, but it looked better after it had been strained to get rid of the bugs and vermin, and anything else that may have fallen in during the distilling process. One sack of grain could be traded for a gallon of Owens' "hooch" (or $10.00 a gallon). Hunters in the area tell of finding old still sites in the draws and overhangs around here. The Owens brothers left the Canyon in the mid-30's, but their memory lingers on.

53.3 Camping beach on left.

N

Power
Lines

Stop

RM
43

Jeep Trail

Bruckett
Canyon

RM
44

Ruggles
(pack)
Grade

46.2

RM
45

RM
46

26m

RM
47

Taylor
(pack)
Grade

49.4

48.1
McCaleb
Cabin

15m

28m

48.3

RM
48

RM
49

Devils Canyon

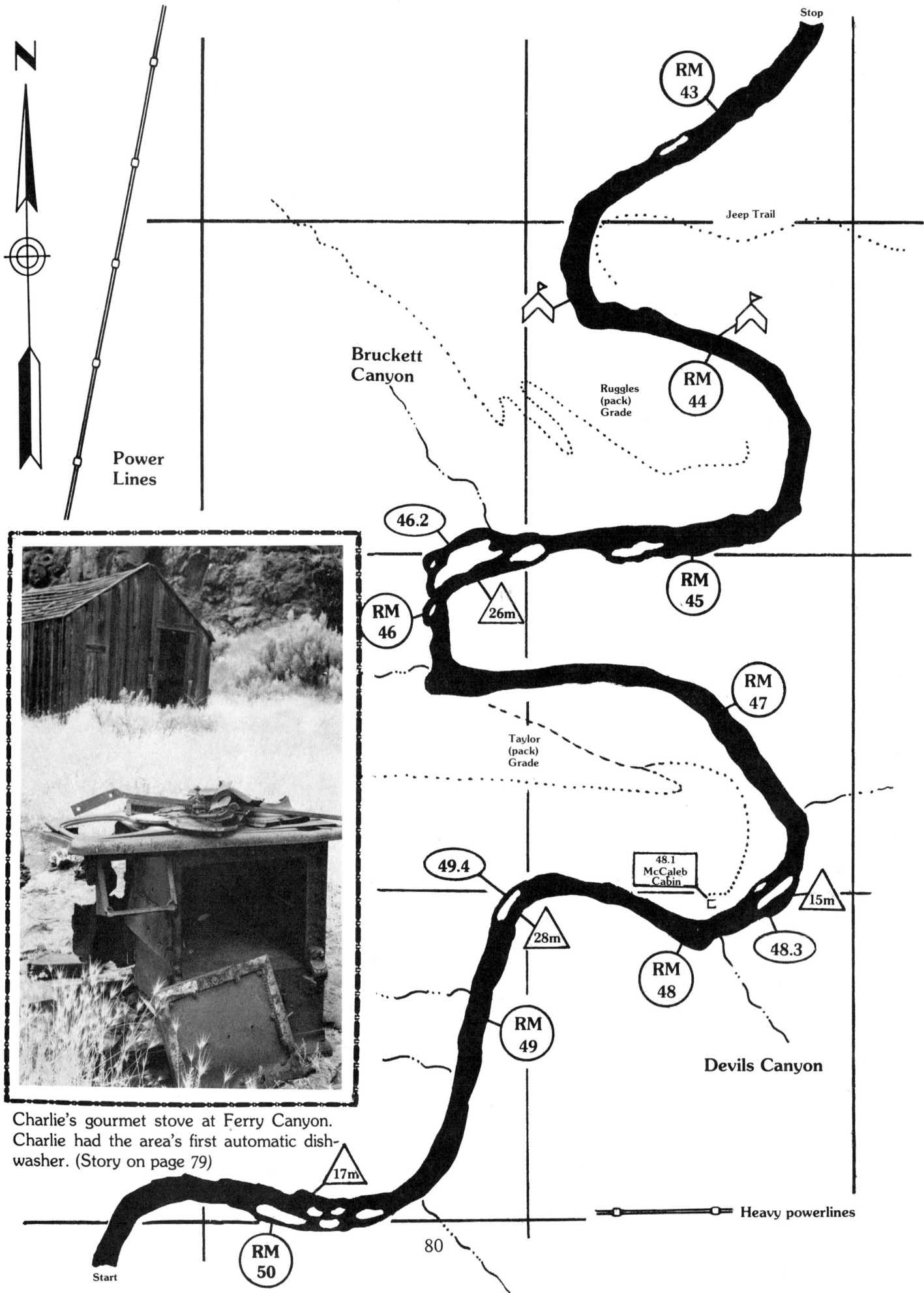

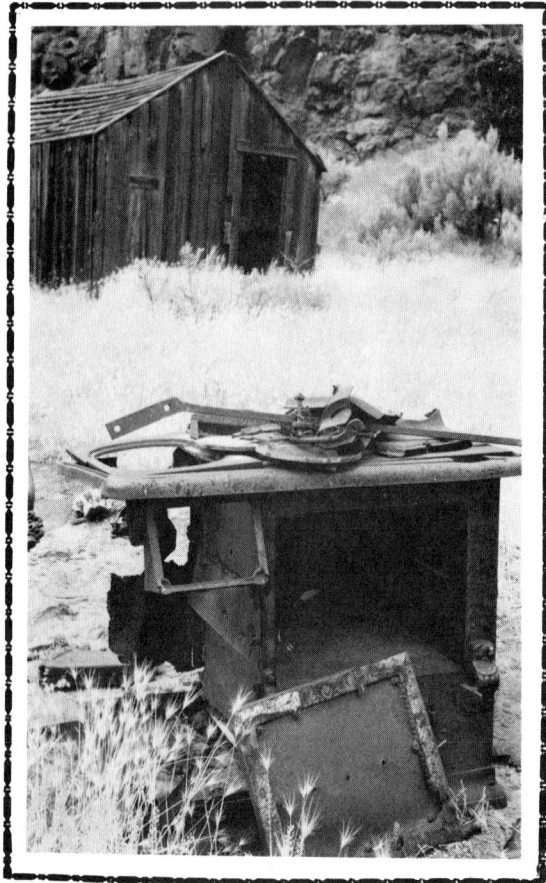

Charlie's gourmet stove at Ferry Canyon.
Charlie had the area's first automatic dish-
washer. (Story on page 79)

17m

⊏⊐━━━⊏⊐ Heavy powerlines

80

RM
50

Start

DRIFT TIME

KAYAK	CANOE	DRIFT BOAT	RAFT	RIVER MILE
9m	10m	12m	15m	52.1
10m	11m	13m	17m	50
				48
16m	18m	21m	27m	48.3
				47
				46
16m	17m	21m	26m	46.2

Island Checkpoint. Two islands on the left side of the channel. The large bar on the right may have water behind it or it may not depending upon the river flow.

At this **Island Checkpoint** the river begins to turn to the right.

Just below river mile 48 are the remains of the old McCaleb cabin built around 1899. This was one of the larger cabins on the river as it had 3 rooms. The sagebrush flat around the cabin was farmed. Across the river Devils Canyon comes in from the right. Near the cabin a spring tooth cultivating device can be seen.

There was a tragic drowning here in February of 1904. Sherman Co. Deputy Sheriff, Charles McCaleb, came to the river near here with 3 or 4 friends to spend several days. McCaleb had a homestead on the Sherman Co. side of the river, as did the other men. One evening McCaleb left the cabin and went downriver to shoot geese. His companions heard several shots, and later when he failed to return went to look for him. On the riverbank they found his clothes, gun and a goose, but no McCaleb. He apparently went in the water after a goose he had shot and drowned in the process. His body was found several days later 50 yards downstream.

The river sweeps to the right and along some red bluffs. There are two islands, the larger island is an **Island Checkpoint.** Take the center channel.

As you drift around from the McCaleb cabin you will notice a road on the hill to the left. This is the Taylor (Pack) Grade. Note how the ravines have been filled in. There is a lot of rock work to keep the road level. In the early days this road would accommodate a small wagon and a team of horses. All the work was done by hand or with horsedrawn tools. Also ahead as you come by mile 47 you will see a double set of powerlines on the ridge in the distance. They run close to the Cottonwood Bridge. You are about 7 miles from the Cottonwood Bridge at this point.

As you head towards mile 46 the river goes into a wider hairpin turn again. Opposite mile 46 is Spring Canyon and below a large island is Bruckett Canyon on the left.

This large island is an **Island Checkpoint.** From here a single set of powerlines can be seen on the ridges as

81

Upper left: Part of a section of wooden water pipe used by the Owens Brothers for an irrigation scheme about 1908. Pipe was part of the Condon Water System until about 1903. Upper right: Old ferry cable tightening apparatus on left bank of river mile 54.3. Ferry ran here from 1893 to about 1920. Lower right: Windmill at Ferry Canyon. Middle left: Are these the boots that Bert killed the rattlesnake with? (See page 79 for story) Below left: Section of completely circular hand built stone corral built behind George's place. Horses were sometimes trained here and held for sale. Stone would not damage horses as wire sometimes does.

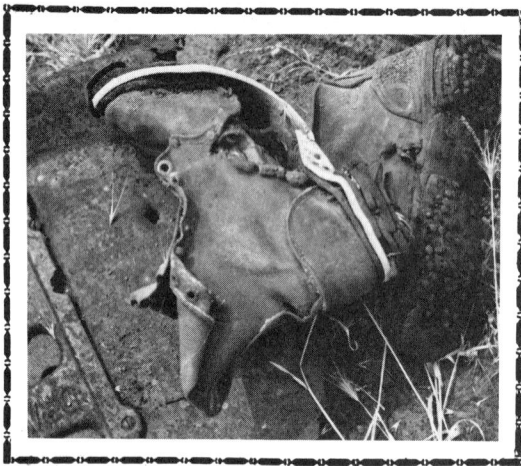

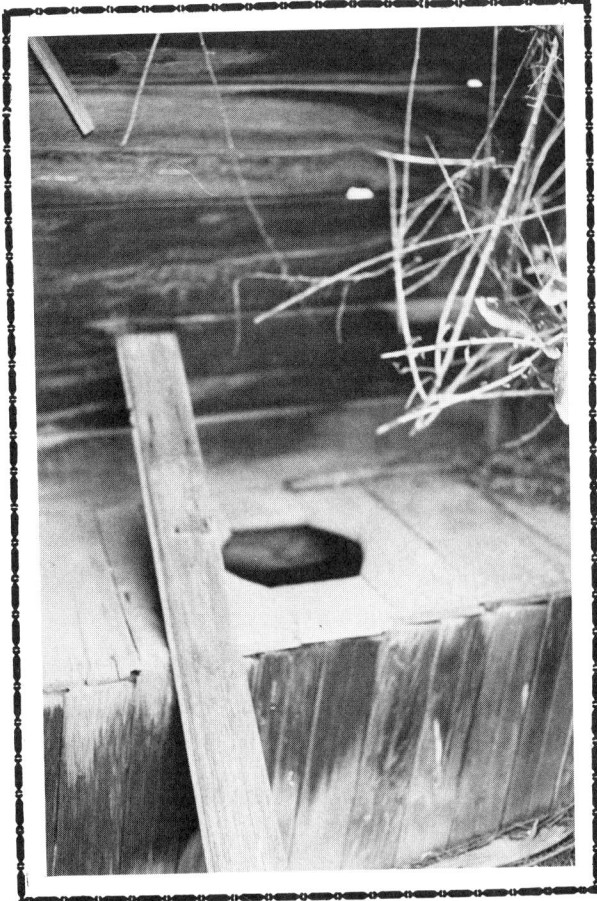

The McCaleb Place: At river mile 48. Left part of the caved in roof inside the cabin. Right: McCaleb's one holer. Note old flowering vine which was common practice around out houses. McCaleb was deputy sheriff of Sherman Co. in 1904 when he was killed hunting geese below here about 1/4 mile. To get a free title to the land a homesteader had to work the land for 5 years before he could lay claim to it. McCaleb did not live here except for an occasional visit and at harvest time to get the crop in. Someone may have worked it for him.

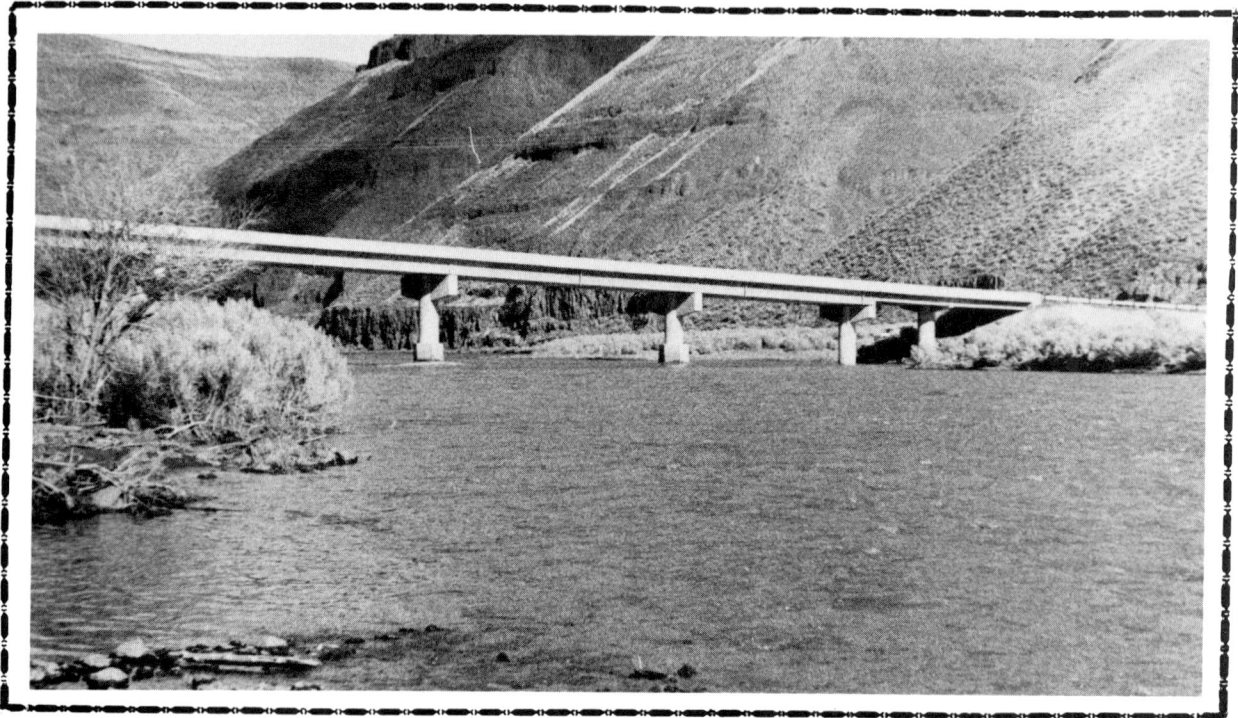

Cottonwood Bridge as seen from upriver. Major take-out point is below bridge to the right. Highway 206 crosses John Day here; Condon is south; Wasco and Biggs Junction are to the north.

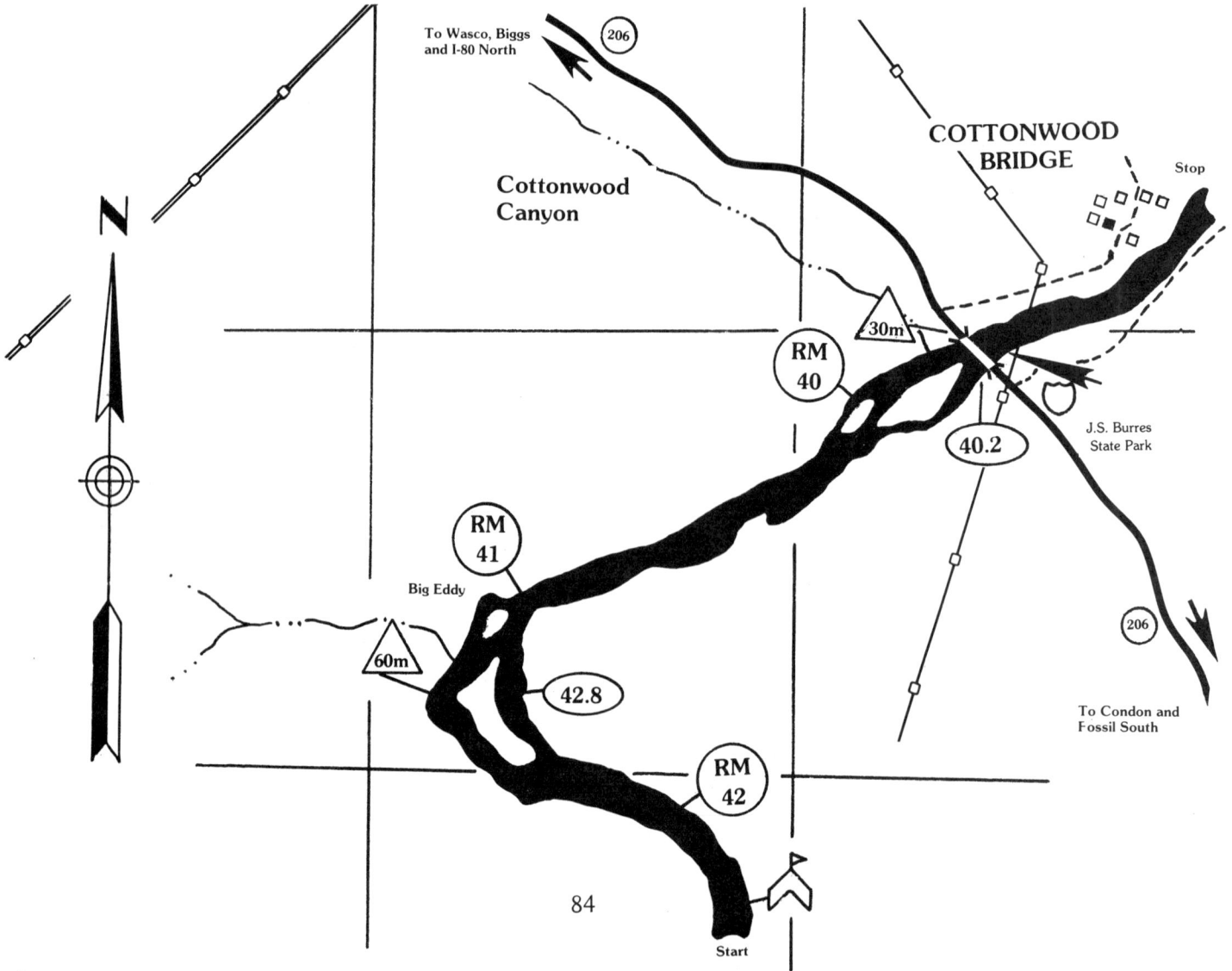

To Wasco, Biggs
and I-80 North

206

Cottonwood
Canyon

COTTONWOOD
BRIDGE

Stop

N

RM
40

30m

40.2

J.S. Burres
State Park

RM
41

Big Eddy

60m

42.8

206

To Condon and
Fossil South

RM
42

84

Start

DRIFT TIME

KAYAK	CANOE	DRIFT BOAT	RAFT	RIVER MILE	
					you look east. These take off from the double lines and parallel highway 206 between Condon and Wasco.
					About 1908 a woman rushed into the sheriff's office and said that her husband had hung himself. (She lived above here on a homestead.) The sheriff and a couple of deputies went out to the place and found the husband with a rope around his neck, tied to a bedpost. She insisted that that was the way she found him. There was no investigation. What a way to go!
				45	On the hill to the left can be seen the Ruggles Pack Grade for jeep or horse.
				44	At mile 44 are two very nice beaches which are 3½ miles from the Cottonwood Bridge.
				44.4	There is a good camping beach on the left.
				43.8	Camping Beach on the right.
37m	41m	48m	60m	42.8	The large island ahead is a **Landmark Checkpoint.** This island will have water around it if the water is high, but only a dry channel at low water on the back side.

About 75 yards downriver from the head of the island is a flat rock with a white arrow on it. This is another elevation mark at 558 feet above sea level. The island is called Big Eddy Island. Near the end is a large swirling basin of water on the left. Don't get into Big Eddy unless you like merry-go-rounds. Below Big Eddy is a smaller island on the left. You are approximately 1 mile from the Cottonwood Bridge.

Charles Kandle lived with his wife on the John Day near the mouth of Cottonwood Creek in the late 1890's. Frank Kimble, a neighbor had a cabin up the canyon and was batching there. Kimble's cabin had been broken into by Indians several times in his absence. Kimble rigged a shotgun to fire if the cabin was entered while he was away, and he left a note outside for any neighbors explaining the danger (he knew the Indians couldn't read). Kandle and his wife came by for a visit, but failed to see the note as it had blown away. Kandle was shot dead as he entered the cabin.

Long Johns & Chickens

The below observations were published by W. W. Weatherford in his book *Over My Shoulder.* Weatherford relates that:

In the early days there were two types of long-johns: the split and lapover kind that never did lap over except when lying on the store counter, or of course you could just give up and wear the drop-door kind that always had the buttons broken off. Either type had

DRIFT TIME

KAYAK	CANOE	DRIFT BOAT	RAFT	RIVER MILE
18m	20m	24m	30m	40.2
				TOTAL

FERRY CANYON TO COTTONWOOD BRIDGE				MILES
1:30	1:40	1:10	2:23	14.1
				TOTAL

30 MILE CREEK TO COTTONWOOD BRDIGE				MILES
5:26	5:14	6:19	8:56	43.9
				TOTAL

BUTTE CREEK TO COTTONWOOD BRIDGE				MILES
7:37	8:07	9:11	12 hr.	58.4
				TOTAL

CLARNO BRIDGE TO COTTONWOOD BRIDGE				MILES
14:20	16:04	18:22	24 hr.	70.6

serious problems with draft control. They itched about the same though and they both turn the hair on your legs the wrong way for an hour or two when you first put them on. That's why most men wore them 24 hours a day.

A few miles east of here in around 1927, Dave Wilson, a rancher, heard something bothering his chickens after he had gone to bed. He got up still in his long-johns (drop-door type with the buttons missing), slipped his shoes on, got his double-barreled shotgun and went pussyfooting out to the hen house. Just as he was sneaking up on the door of the hen house with his gun at the ready, expecting anything from skunk to cougar, Dave's old dog stuck his cold nose right in Dave's bare behind! Dave said they had fried chicken, boiled chicken, chicken and dumplings, chicken soup and lots of feathers, but no more eggs for a long, long time.

There are usually two islands just above the bridge. Go between them for the main channel.

The Cottonwood Bridge is a **Landmark Checkpoint.** If you are beaching here there is a landing beach to the right.

We hope you have enjoyed your drift and please carry out your trash. Good luck and good boating.

INDEX